Chains Falling

A Study of Rebellion and Redemption in Hosea

Jamy Fisher

Be Blessed!
Psalm 107:2
Jamy Fisher

CROSSBOOKS
PUBLISHING

CrossBooks™
A Division of LifeWay
1663 Liberty Drive
Bloomington, IN 47403
www.crossbooks.com
Phone: 1-866-879-0502

First published by CrossBooks 7/21/2011

ISBN: 978-1-4627-0536-8 (sc)
ISBN: 978-1-4627-0537-5 (hc)

Cover and author photography by Julie Busler.
Cover Model, Sarah Barham.

Printed in the United States of America

This book is printed on acid-free paper.

Dedicated to those I teach who encouraged me to believe that our lessons together should be shared.

Contents

Introduction - How to use this Study   ix

Week 1 – Prophet Hosea, Husband Hosea   1

Week 2 – God's People Passion   17

Week 3 – Redemption   37

Week 4 – The Case Against God's People   55

Week 5 – Coming Home   71

Week 6 – Walk on with Repentance on Your Mind   89

Small Group Guide   109

Favorite Recipes   115

Works Cited   121

Introduction - How to use this Study

Thank you for joining me on this journey through Hosea. It will be an exciting ride! Let me just warn you; *Hosea is challenging.* A few years ago I was struck by a single verse from Hosea that showed up in another study. When I looked all around this verse there were some scary things going on. I decided I had to learn what this book was all about. I was simply amazed and changed forever by what I learned. I taught what I was learning to my Bible Study ladies. Every Wednesday they stuck with me as we traversed the verses from my list of bullet point lessons. This book is those bullet points written into an interactive study. It will present some things that we'd much rather just skip over, in fact we usually do. If you take a shallow look at the book of Hosea it seems that God is rejecting His people, even that He wants to hurt them – but just the opposite is true! The part of His character that reacts to our rebellion can be scary, but we'll learn it's only because He loves us so much. Seeing the depth of His grief and anger at our easy abandonment of Him will help us develop an attachment to redemption that is life-changing and strong. We will delve into parts of God's heart that will be brand new to you, they were to me. There will be questions that come up, it's OK to ask them! I trust God's Word so much and I know that every second you spend studying or struggling with it is an investment in spiritual growth that only God can generate. *And I know He will!*

This Bible Study is designed for 6 weeks of study. Ideally you should get your Bible Study Buddies together and talk about what you've learned each week. There will be plenty to discuss! Every lesson is one I learned while studying Hosea at my dining room table. I wish we could be there together talking about what we're learning.

You'll need a couple of things to make the most of this study:
- *Bible*. Preferably a Study Bible with some great notes to help you out when we get to the *"whaaaat?"* parts of this study. I use my ginormous and beloved ESV (English Standard Version) Study Bible.
- *Access to various Bible translations.* I use Biblegateway.com on my computer. When you are studying the Bible, especially difficult passages, this is a very valuable tool. If you will read the passage in at least three, preferably four or five translations from different ends of the translation spectrum you generally are able to get down to the intended meaning. Here's a short lesson on Bible translations. The Bible was originally written in mostly Hebrew and Greek. Scholars have translated those texts into English for regular gals like us. Some translations are quite literal which means the scholars translated each word from the original language into a corresponding English word whenever possible. Examples are New American Standard (NASB), New King James (NKJV), and English Standard Version (ESV). Some are less literal meaning the scholars took an entire phrase from the original language and translated it into English. These are often more easy to understand. Some examples are New International Version (NIV) and on the most loosely translated end of the spectrum New Living Translation (NLT) and The Message (MSG). This is my advice on translations. Own a great Study Bible in a more literal translation; but read from other translations OFTEN and especially when you are having trouble understanding something.

I mentioned biblegateway.com. I have a tab on my computer set to this website. When I want to read a passage in various translations I click on "passage lookup" and a search blank pops up. Underneath are 5 slots where you can choose translations. Mine is set to ESV, NASB, NIV, AMP, and MSG. When I hit the search button, whatever passage I have entered comes up in all five translations. By the time I read *thoughtfully* through all these wordings, I have opened up my heart and mind for God to drop His intended meaning right in. If you are not a computer person, make the investment and buy two or three cheap paperback versions in various translations so you can practice this same thing.

- *Journal.* I am a reluctant journaler, but I believe it makes a big difference in your interaction with what you are learning. Each day will end with a Journal Prompt. Finish your day's study by writing the question in your journal (plain spiral or fancy with flowers – your call). Take a deep breath, reflect on what you learned in the day's study, and interact. You will notice that some of them read like a third grade creative writing assignment. For example, Day 2 of Week 1 says, *Gomer's story leaves me feeling......* Some of you will want to write, *"angry"* or *"like she's a loser."* Go a little deeper. These prompts are intentionally simple and open so that you can interact with GOD, not me, as you write. Turn these journal entries into prayers somewhere along the way. Try it and see what happens.
- *Time away from crazy life.*
- *A fresh brain.* Some of this stuff will seriously require a "thinking cap" (as Mrs. Van, my 6th grade teacher used to say – she'd even make us buckle it under our chin).

Here we go. Buckle up, I can't wait!
Jamy

Week 1 – Prophet Hosea, Husband Hosea

Day 1: Hosea Introduced

"Hosea put it well:
I'll call nobodies and make them somebodies;
I'll call the unloved and make them beloved.
In the place where they yelled out, "You're nobody!"
they're calling you 'God's living children.'" Romans 9:25 The
Message

Hosea comes upon the scene in 770 BC. This is a time of material
prosperity for God's people. King Jeroboam has extended the
kingdom. He has led them to experience military victory and
safety from their enemies (2 Kings 14:23-27). For the first time
since Solomon was king over a unified kingdom, Israel's borders
have been reclaimed and all seems to be smooth sailing. Were
you to look in on them they appear successful and religious.
But God has never been into appearances and He knows that
the spiritual bankruptcy of the people has not changed with
their material prosperity. He knows that captivity is just around
the corner if they reject His call. And when God's people forget
Him He is always faithful to send His Word, to tell them the
truth and call them to return to Him. These are the themes of
the book of Hosea: man's bent toward and God's intolerance
of idolatry and God's great and wide redeeming love. Only
God could find a solution to the problems we create. Only God
loves us enough to even try. Enter the first two characters of
our story: Hosea and his wife, Gomer. Their story is told in the
first three chapters of the book of Hosea.

Read Hosea 1:1-2 and Romans 9:25. These are the places
where Hosea is mentioned by name. Can you find the meaning
of Hosea's name? It isn't in the text, but might be in your
footnotes.

"The name "Hosea" comes from the same verb as "Joshua" and "Jesus" meaning to save or deliver."[1]

How important is the meaning of this name as you consider Hosea's surroundings?

Hosea was a real man who married a real woman in obedience to God's call. He was a prophet, which must rank at the top of the list for difficult jobs. The prophet Isaiah walked around naked and barefoot for three years (Isaiah 20:3-5), and Ezekiel ate food cooked with human excrement (Ezekiel 4). Seriously, I don't think many young Israelites were hanging out at the "prophet booth" on career fair day. The prophet didn't often get the privilege of leading the people through the joyous recitations of the pleasant parts of the Scriptures. Instead, he got the harrowing task of telling them the truth about their lifestyles and the condition of their lives inside out. Correcting cranky, rebellious, spoiled, religious people who don't like to be bossed – this was Hosea's job. His marriage was not easy; it was the "tragedy of a good marriage that began well and went bad."[2] And, it is also part of our story with God. God is serious and creative about getting the attention of His people. He knows that we are moved by a love story. He created us that way and uses romance to draw us to Him still. He called Hosea to a difficult marriage to illustrate His own love relationship with His people. That fact is stated emphatically in the book of Hosea. Here, in Hosea 1, is one of my favorite images of Hosea. I imagine Hosea's heart swelling and his throat tightening as he is filled with longing to share God's Words with the people. I'm sure the burden of their denial of God was something that already caused him great pain. He is listening carefully with a holy desperation to hear God's voice and he does. See him hearing God's call for the first time.

---

1   (ESV Study Bible), 1623.
2   ESV Study Bible, 1623

Read Hosea 1:2 and summarize God's call to Hosea. It would be helpful to read it in two or three versions.

God calls him to a marriage that will break his heart and risk his unborn children. Do you imagine he thought he'd misheard? I wonder if he would rather have been called to walk around naked or eat poop. Some of you have endured the splintering pain of an affair in your marriage. What if God had allowed you to see that path before you walked through it? Would you have chosen it knowing only that through the pain there would be redemption and God's glory?

Have you ever asked God for a glimpse like this? Why do we do this?

Read Hosea's reaction and note it:

Nothing fancy, no bargaining or counter-offers, just obedience. Do you see why this is one of my favorite pictures of him in the book? He trusted God with great courage knowing the obstacles ahead would be insurmountable without Him. He was willing for the sake of God's Words.

There is a great list of characteristics of prophets in my Study Bible. Take a look at these:

1. The prophets assert that God has spoken through them.
2. The prophets affirm that God chose Israel for covenant relationship.
3. The prophets most often report that the majority of Israel has sinned against their God and His standards for their relationship.
4. The prophets warn that judgment will eradicate sin.
5. The prophets promise that renewal lies beyond the day of punishment that has occurred already in history and beyond the coming day that will bring history as we know it to a close.[3]

Now I know this is a little academic for our first day together, but these assumptions are important as we wade through a difficult book. In this study we will talk about the reality of Hosea's marriage to Gomer. Then we will dive straight into the redeeming love relationship God offers as deeply as you will go with me: this is number two on the prophet list above. Then we will courageously hear the grief and wrath of God aimed toward sin: this is number three and number four. Our last consideration will be God's forgiveness and hope: number five. Perhaps you've heard parts of these prophetic books (much of what is between Psalms and Matthew) used to accuse God of being harsh and unloving. How can a loving God say such things? How can He do such things? Have you ever dealt with questions like that, what were they?

---

3   (ESV Study Bible), 1230-1231.

When Christians can't answer these questions we tend to pick out the warm fuzzy verses and ignore the rest. As I guide you through Hosea, I have no fancy credentials to give you here. I have no plans to wow you with my intellect in these verses. I just wrote the word poop, for heaven's sake! I am a pastor's wife, a momma, and a Bible Teacher. If you leave this study and don't feel that Hosea was written for you, if you don't walk away convinced that God's love is greater than anything else you have loved back, if you don't walk away from this study more confident in God's Word with chains falling as you walk into your future, then this effort is a failure in my eyes. I love God's Word and believe that ALL of it is for ALL of us. No smarty-pants efforts here, just real attachment to God and His Word.

Journal Prompt: The things that make me feel intimidated about studying Hosea are....

Day 2: Gomer Introduced

Gomer. She is often portrayed as a prostitute sought out by Hosea for the sole purpose of teaching Israel a lesson. Most likely that isn't who she is in the beginning.

Read Hosea chapter 1 and chapter 3. These are the chapters that chronicle Hosea's marriage. Write down everything you learn about Gomer.

We only know a few things for sure. She was chosen by Hosea. She marries him and has a child. Here's a place where I wish so much for more details. What happened to Gomer to bring her to this crossroad? When I opened my internet browser this morning, the lead story was a woman who wrote a book about why she left her husband and two sons to pursue her own life. Could this be Gomer's story? Did she feel too tied down by family life? Had her mother made her feel she was a burden or her father made her believe she was invisible and unloved? Was she just nuts? Did she even love Hosea? We also know that somewhere between the birth of her first and second baby she becomes an adulteress (2:2, 2:5, 3:1).

What is your first honest reaction to Gomer?

 Brave

We may gasp and judge or shake our heads in confusion. Maybe you understand it very well and this story tears off some carefully cared for soul band-aids. It is difficult to get close to this type of abandonment, but let me just assure you that going deep with Gomer is your first jumping off point to understanding anew the depth of God's grace. When you were little and wanted to jump into the deep end of the swimming pool, wasn't it easier if you had a friend's hand to hold? Hold onto my hand and let's jump together. After Gomer's first baby is born she has two more children with other men and most likely leaves her family to chase other loves, (2:5,7, 3:1,3) coming home only when desperate (2:7) and only to leave again. If we continue to follow the parallels of God's comparison between His people and Gomer, we see that during these difficult years she receives gifts from Hosea, but doesn't acknowledge they were from him (2:8). I imagine Hosea searching for Gomer with three little kids in tow. He can't make her come home but he does take gifts for her and leaves them for her even though she doesn't know it. She chases and sleeps with many other men and she becomes involved with the prevalent idol worship common in her culture. Eventually, she becomes a slave (3:2).

What might've led her to this desperate situation? Why do you think Gomer didn't just go home?

According to my Study Bible, the going rate for a slave during the last half of the 8th century was thirty shekels. Did you see how much Gomer cost? Fifteen shekels. She became a half price slave (3:2). Gomer had sought and fought for freedom and found the exact opposite because she trusted a lie.

Read Hosea 1:2 and 3:1. Gomer is the unfaithful wife. According to these verses, who does she represent?

God used Gomer's real life example to show the devastation in the lives of His people. We also are God's people and His promises and warnings to us are very true. Idolatry may look different in our days, but it is just as deadly to our spiritual lives. If you are feeling a little bit bloodied and bruised from Gomer's current enslavement, hang in there. She is loved and she does come home. But just like Gomer has to learn the truth about what she'd been chasing, so do we.

Journal Prompt: Gomer's story leaves me feeling......

like Hosea get exaushted not as much as I thought,

Day 3: Idolatry- Believing the Lie

Idolatry is defined in The Holman Bible Dictionary as, *"a physical or material image or form **representing a reality** or being considered divine and thus an **object of worship**."*[4] I find this definition very fascinating. We tend to think we are free from idolatry because we don't worship little handheld wooden idols like we've seen in pictures or read about in the Bible. Rewrite the parts of the definition that I've underlined redefining idolatry in your own words:

Read Hosea 2 (as well as the footnotes if you have a Study Bible) and answer these questions keeping in mind that God is already making the comparisons between Gomer and His people.

How did Gomer do these things? In other words, what did she make as an object of worship that only represented a reality?

Now, after you've thought about that and written it out, think about this: how do you do the same thing? What are some things that you've made an object of worship that only represent a reality?

This will become a key part of our study. As much as we long to identify with Hosea, the beginnings of our journey to redemption lie with Gomer. If you can't find the Gomer in your own life then you will miss the miracle of redemption that is

---

4   (Butler), 686.

yet to come. If you glossed over the previous two questions, go back and reconsider them.

Read these verses and note what they teach.
Hosea 2:8, 13

Proverbs 3:5-6

Isaiah 43:10-12

Journal Prompt: God might accuse me of having an idolatrous heart toward Him because I give too much attention to the following people or things......

Lord, show me what it is I give my attention too!
Is it my clothes, or just outer appearance? Lord I want to grow in You' teach me how I can grow! Give me wisdom!

Day 4: Idolatry, Worshipping the Lie

We learned yesterday that part of idolatry is belief that a lie is true. What was the second part of the definition we learned? Write it here:

being considered an object of worship

To worship something means I adore it, I am aware of its presence when it's close and miss it when it's far away. I long to have it with me and spend time invested deeply in understanding and knowing how it operates.........you get the idea? We worship people, things, ourselves, achievements; both good and bad.

According to what you just read, who or what do you worship? *Shopping*

Read Isaiah 44:9-20. What do you think is the main idea? You can summarize it in smaller parts to start with, but try to get it down to one or two sentences.

We say and act like having things is not a big deal. But we put more + more time into it to make it wonderful

Choose one part of our passage that challenges you the most. Now look at your cross-references for that verse if you have them in your Bible. Usually in Study Bibles these will be in the margin. As I'm reading along there will be little letter subscripts in the verses. If I look to the margin the verse number will be listed there with the corresponding letter subscripts. Your Bible might have similar references. Write down the references given and look them up. Write down what you learn. If you've never done this before or don't have cross-references here's some help. For verse 20 the cross-references for the phrase "Is there not a lie in my right hand?" are Psalm 144:8 and Romans 1:25. Feel free to use mine....it goes with the next part.

We always think our way to go is the best or that it really doesn't matter if I let my gard down for a bit. but it does matter. "We have exchanged the troth of God with a lie"

Did you see the part at the end (verse 20) where idolatry kept them from being able to recognize lies? Sounds a lot like "representing a reality" from our definition yesterday. I don't like to be misled, I don't like to be lied to, or find out that something I trusted was a deception. God's Word tells me that idolatry does just that. If you want to have a life that is characterized by truth and a correct understanding of God you must get rid of idols. That habit, relationship, addiction – whatever it is, it must go. I imagine that Gomer believed little lies in the beginning, but little lies always turn our focus on ourselves and blind us as they become bigger and bigger. Eventually they will enslave. Wherever you are on this path, don't go any further without asking God for wisdom to recognize any lies you've believed and anything you've put in a place of worship reserved for Him alone.

Journal Prompt: My favorite verse from today is: because......

Verse 20 " He feeds on Ashes" We know what we are doing is bad we just can't let it go. God help me to let it go.

Day 5: The Children

The last characters in our story are often overlooked, but they have a powerful chapter to add. They are Gomer and Hosea's children. They are given prophetic names as was the custom when Hosea and Gomer lived. Read Hosea 1:4, 1:6, 1:9 and list the names of the children in the list below along with the name meanings. Most likely only Jezreel is fathered by Hosea, I've filled in his info for you. His name means "scattered."[5] Now add a huge dash with the word "becomes" right next to the name meanings as a reminder that these symbolic names are not permanent. Yes, that is a weird instruction, but do it anyway, it will make sense soon.

Jezreel: Scattered **BECOMES** – *Planted*[6]

Lo-Ruhamah:

Lo-Ammi:

Two sons and a daughter. Some of you have families that look just like this one. You can see the faces of these little ones born close in age; two brothers with a sister right in the middle. One of the most difficult parts of the book of Hosea for me is the naming of Hosea and Gomer's children. I have such a hard time with God allowing these children to be named Unloved and Not His. I take comfort in the fact that these kiddos grew up with a very godly father who was sure to communicate their role in proclaiming God's message to His people. By the end of the book I've never been more convinced in God's absolute and relentless love and I'm sure that these children knew God removed the "NOT" from their names. But still, these are just little babies – paying a price for their Mama's sin. Although this

---

5   (Boice), 17.
6   (Boice), 20.

is a part of life, it's not a part of life that is beyond God or His mighty saving arm. For some of you this is familiar, you know the pain of paying for the mistakes of a wayward or unwise parent. For a moment let's focus on what the Bible teaches about God's loving character. He allowed the names of Hosea's children to reflect what a season of rebellion can do.

Read these verses making a list in your journal of everything you learn about God's love.
- Psalm 103:13

- Psalm 100:5

- Psalm 136

So, now that you've read them and made your list, look it over and answer the next question.

Is there ever a time that these verses are not true of Him?

When life looks like God has permanently stamped "UNLOVED" on your hand, remember these verses. It is true that God loves you as a tender father loves a precious daughter. It is true that His love endures throughout the generations. If you are on either side of a Gomer-sized family shattering mistake let the truth that God's love endures throughout the generations be a beacon of hope for you. Say it to yourself 26 times, that's how many times He repeats it in Psalm 136. His love endures!

Let's look at this subject from another angle. Have you ever had a season when you blamed God for calling you unloved or not His, when really it was your own sin that put you there? If you are in such a season because of your own sin or that of another, please take heart in knowing that God takes no delight in your pain, but He can miraculously use it to make you stronger and draw you closer to Him.

Before we take one more step into this study read Hosea 2:1. What does God say to the sister? What does God say to the brothers? Go back to the original list you made of these children's names. Next to the "becomes" that you have already written, add the new names that God gives them.

What did you see?

Our own disobedience or that of another can cast over us for a season the titles "Not Loved" and "Not God's". Although God allows this, it is never His design or His delight! Hear me in this! If you have, through your own destructive choices or those of another, been living under a "NOT", why stay there? Can you trust God to rename you? Because He's already done it.

Journal Prompt: The name I most often live under is...... God calls me........

Week 2 – God's People
Passion

Day 1: The Godly Yet

The book of Hosea is kind of a downer. It's heavy and depressing and full of a bunch of difficult images that we don't appreciate....at all! Remember this is a book written to offer correction to a very wayward bunch. But there are a few places, and I will be VERY quick to point them out, where God's hope is the main attraction. This day highlights one of those spots. It is the central teaching of this book of God's Word. I call it The Godly Yet.

Read Hosea 1:9-2:1 to get the surroundings of the Godly Yet. What is the first word of Hosea 1:10?

Right in the middle of Hosea 1:10 is a phrase that most of our English translations don't even have. According to my favorite Word Study Dictionary this verse reads more literally, "Yet the number of the children of Israel shall be as the sand of the sea, which cannot be measured nor numbered; **and it shall come to pass,** that in the place where it was said unto them, ye are not my people, there it shall be said unto them, Ye are the sons of the living God."[7] That phrase in the middle "And it shall come to pass" is "hayah". It means "to breathe; it means to exist, to be, to come to pass; to be done, to happen, to be finished."[8]

In most of our modern Bibles, it's just a very plain word that connects the thoughts. But in reality it is God's creative breath. Did you see all the ugliness of Hosea and Gomer's story? Do you see the damage that her destructive choices have caused? God does! He recognizes it and calls it what it is. In fact throughout the book of Hosea God uses very descriptive and disgusting word pictures that take several verses at a time. The beauty of the Godly Yet is not that God overlooks the death in our sinful

---

7   (Zodhiates), 2141.
8   (Zodhiates), 2311.

choices. The beauty of the Godly Yet is that right in the middle of it He breathes and calls something new into existence and finishes the story.

Where does God do this? Return to our passage for today and write down the WHERE of the renaming process.

One of my favorite things in the Godly YET is that God does this right where the whole thing unraveled in the first place, "in the place where it was said to them."

One of my daughters has beautiful curly auburn hair. When she was younger, I would pull the front part of her hair (the fall into the eyes part) into a little top-right side ponytail. One day she became curious about cutting her hair and decided to cut off her little top ponytail. When she did, her hair fell into a little fuzzy crooked row of red bangs over her forehead. Many of you know from experience that bangs are not typically great ideas for curly hair. She took care of her mess and went on with her day assuming everything was fine. I took one look at her and asked her what she had done to her hair. I will never forget the look of genuine confusion on her face. She had carefully handled this herself. When she saw the offending hair in her hand she dealt with it herself. She threw the hair with the ponytail holder still attached behind her dresser where I found it later. She was offended that I could tell by looking at her that she had done something wrong. Don't we do this with God? We know that the idolatry we cherish isn't right, but we handle it ourselves throwing any evidence behind our dressers. Then we march out before God with our crooked fuzzy bangs and puff up in arrogance at Him when He reminds us that they are crooked and ugly and not at all what He intended for us. Just like Israel you are standing at the crossroads of verse 9 and verse 10. What word connects verse 9 and 10?

Take the step of faith and trust toward God's kind and alive and transforming YET.

The "Godly Yet" describes God's patient way of telling us the truth, while never letting go. A few years ago when I was first studying and teaching Hosea, I was a part of the closing ceremony for an event at Oklahoma Baptist University, where students and faculty read aloud through the New Testament in 24 hours. I got there just in time to hear the last few chapters of Revelation. Now, keep in mind that I had Hosea on the brain and then I got tossed into Revelation. And guess what? Jesus was there fulfilling every need and promise that was uttered back in Hosea! It was an amazingly humbling and eye-opening experience. God is terribly hurt by our rebellion and He never glosses it over. He calls sin exactly what it is and doesn't try to make us feel better about ourselves when we're compromising. YET, (this is the Godly Yet part), *Jesus never ever leaves us there*. Did I leave my sweet daughter alone with her massacred bangs? No, we went to see Mrs. Lori and she did her best to fix and blend and remind us that they would grow out. This is the Godly YET. Wherever your life is the messiest, where the nastiest secret hides, and most closely guarded wound festers, God sees and He calls it the ugly it is. YET, He never leaves you there alone with no way to heal, with no hope that it will grow out. He might give you a long leash while you're fighting Him, but He is never content to reject you. He just can't stand it. So He waits and whispers His truth over you and tells you the truth about the evil in your choices (often with graphic and unappreciated candor and detail) and reassures you of His love and your true identity and tells you the truth some more. Right in the midst of the carnage, He breathes life. The formula goes something like this: God says, "Here's the sin I see........*(fill in the blank)*.......and this is what consequences it will bring........ *(another blank)*.......YET, I love you and I will redeem even this in you to bring you closer to me and make you so certain in your redeemed identity that you are astonishingly effective as you represent Me in the darkness around you."

Draw a diagram illustrating the Godly YET. OK, I usually hate to do this in Bible Studies and skip all drawing questions – but just try it. If you are super artistic you can do pictures, if not you can just add words.

YET

I want you to have this visual picture of the Godly YET. This concept has transformed my spiritual insight. I see it everywhere in Scripture now. I'll be studying for a Sunday School lesson or reading a story to my 3 year old or listening to a new song on the radio or listening to a precious one in my Bible Study share what she's learning and there it is – the beautiful merciful Godly YET. Even now my heart swells with gratitude for this understanding of His love for me. When I begin to bristle toward the things God did or does or allows that make NO sense to me I remember that I may be looking at the first part of the Godly YET.....and the best is still YET.

Journal Prompt: The Godly Yet means.......

Day 2: Achor

Read Hosea chapter 2:2-13. How would you describe the "mother" in these verses? Don't get hung up in God's reaction to her, we'll face that in a later chapter. For now just react to her.

Can you see her reliance only on her senses? She does what is in front of her chasing after the next great feeling and never finding it. We were created for more than feral running after pleasure. This type of chase only leads to trouble.

Read Hosea 2:14-15. This is one of those Hopeful spots in the book. Remember, I told you I would point them out! God says in verse 15 that He will make the Valley of Achor into a Door of Hope. Notice that the word Achor means Trouble. It was a bad name and a very bad story. You can read the story in Joshua 7. One man's disobedience cost him and his entire family their lives and terrified an entire nation. That was very nearly true for Gomer and is true also for us. The Israelites used the word Achor to describe a time of tragic correction to a rebellious heart.

When we were in college my husband Todd and I went on a mission trip with a group from our Baptist Student Union to the Ukraine. One of the culinary discoveries we made while we were there was a uniquely mild and soft white cheese. We often ate sandwiches made with this yummy stuff especially if we were traveling. It was easy to pack. During one of our last days in country, the cheese Todd ate must've gotten too warm or been a little old because after he ate it he got deathly and disgustingly ill. It was right before we were all heading home and left a very bad taste in his mouth, pun intended. He arrived home after this amazing trip still pale from his encounter with this Ukrainian Cheese. To this day, if I say the words "Ukrainian Cheese" it will cause him to make a fake gagging face. Words are funny that way.

Do you have some symbolic words like this is your life? I have a few of a more serious and secretive nature. Some are people's names and some are specific places, all are regrettable and the memories associated with them usually make me cringe. Does it astonish you at all to know that God changes Trouble into Hope? If not, you just need to think about it a little longer.

Read the following verses and make a list of what you learn about God's abilities.

Jeremiah 32:27

Romans 5:3-5

What does Isaiah 65:10 tell us about Achor?

I've been teaching women and teenagers for almost all of the 18 years I've been in ministry. During that time I have taught and re-taught many DVD Bible Studies. When I repeat a study I will often use the same study book, making new notes. Recently I started a study for a third time over the course of several years. I got to a question that had been answered for the first time six years ago. The entry said this, "I'm still sad over the loss of baby---seeking God's plans for my time, He keeps sending me back to just knowing Him. I want to see Him in my now, but also in my future!" The second entry written right next to it was dated 18 months later. It said, "As I re-teach this we are making plans to adopt." The baby lost early in 2005 was my fourth heaven baby. I was so weary from trying to find understanding and peace about the size of my family. Some of you know there are a lot of exhausting decisions that go along with this type of trial. I was so sad and remained so for several months. I felt like I had served my time in the miscarriage holding pen. I wanted a big wonderful family. I was scared to get pregnant and scared not to. I felt guilty for not just being ok since I had two healthy children – and I now knew how miraculous it was that my body had cooperated to give them life. I was just tired and discouraged. I didn't know that 18 months later a little girl would be conceived. Her birth mother had a different path, no less painful than mine. Although we didn't know the specifics, God put the desire to find this little girl firmly in the heart of my husband, and I followed eagerly. Through a bizarre, hair-graying, adrenaline and wonder-filled next 9 months, our baby girl was added to our family where God knew from the beginning of time she belonged.

This is God turning Trouble into Hope and it delights Him. Would I have weathered those 18 months better had I known that our Anna was waiting at the end? I'm not telling, because I suspect not......I don't really know. The lesson of it all makes me cringe a little, and then smile a lot.

Now think about this, when has God changed your Achor into Hope?

If He hasn't done this for you yet, just keep in mind that He can because as you continue to walk with Him, He will. Maybe you're currently facing a Trouble Valley time where hope seems impossible to find. If that's you, rest in knowing that this type of transformation is God's specialty and something only He can do. Yes, this is a perfect time to close with a prayer of thanks in your journal.

Journal Prompt: Thank You God for turning trouble into hope when You.........

Day 3: God's Grief

God is passionate. There are so many parts of the imagery in Hosea that are difficult for us. We often miss this about God. The grief He experiences over Israel's rebellion is painful and He articulates it profoundly! This book would be cleaner and easier to read if God didn't care so much or if He were just interested in controlling and punishing His rebellious children. Have you ever been nearby on the worst day of a person's life? When they hear the news of a tragic death of a loved one or are in the midst of a real crisis, not the trivial things we elevate? Isn't there part of you that just wants to close the door quickly so you don't feel their pain - a part that wants to run the other way because you have intruded on an unimaginable loss?

When I was growing up we had some family friends that were dear to us. There were three generations in this close family. The young adult daughter was substitute teaching in my grade school class one day, and I felt so special because I had known her my whole life. Several years older than me, she had been one of the teenagers that I watched and loved.....one who made me want to grow up. This particular day she was in our class and her daddy (who I knew should've been across town teaching school) came and called her out to the hallway, looking very serious. Feeling entitled to join the family meeting, I crept over to the doorway to see what was happening and say hello. As I peeked through the crack in the door I saw her face as her daddy told her that her precious Grandmother had died unexpectedly. I will never forget the look of that first violent crack of tragedy as it crashed over her face. I ran back to my seat, heart breaking with each wild thump, wishing I hadn't seen that grief and hoping it would never happen to me.

Although God is not surprised or powerless, as we are in these situations, His immovable restraint to always give us the choice to love Him or another often causes Him grief. Please read the end of that sentence again because it is painfully long. His immovable restraint to always give us the choice to love Him or another often causes Him grief. The book of Hosea is a glimpse through the "crack of the door" so to speak, as God feels the tragedy of His children's rebellion. The depth of His pain is seen in these pictures of adultery and death.

As you read Hosea, can you feel God's emotions? How would you describe them?

Let's look ahead in our study a few chapters and see a glimpse of God's raw emotion. What questions does He ask in Hosea 11:8?

Keeping in mind that "Ephraim" and "Israel" are group names for God's people and apply to you, what does this say about his attachment to you?

Read Jeremiah 2:2, 13, 32 and note what you learn about God's emotional reaction to our sin.

Look now at Jesus' reaction to this same predicament. Matthew 23:37 and Luke 13:34 both record this "crack in the door" moment. Read them and jot down what He says.

What does God want to do but is unable to?

Is God truly not powerful enough to force us to obey Him? He could, but He chooses not to. I just can't get my head around this – if I could make my kids obey me I would, in a heartbeat, without getting up from the couch. God doesn't love you out of obligation and He doesn't want you to love Him back out of fear. He wants you to see you are loved, to be wooed and convinced, and then to come running to Him because you couldn't possibly belong anywhere else. I think this is one of the foundational lessons for us when we study the rebel – return – rebel – return pattern of the Israelites in the Old Testament. He won't make you do right and He won't make you love Him. And He won't stop loving you no matter what.

Does this challenge what you've thought about God to this point in your life?

Ephesians 4:17-32 holds some amazing gems on grieving the Holy Spirit. Read it and find the verse that specifically references God's grief, then take special note of what might cause it. It would be helpful to read this entire passage in several versions.

Look back at the notes you've made about the Triune God (that means God the Father, Jesus, and the Holy Spirit) experiencing grief. Answer this question before you move onto your journal entry: Is it my actions or something else that grieves God?

Journal Prompt: God, I didn't know that you felt grief when…..

Day 4: Exclamatory Blessedness Waiting

I cannot begin to tell you how crushed I would be if this were the end of the story. What if you knew that God loved you and passionately wanted to have a relationship with you, but there was no way for that to happen? Enter another Godly Yet. Remember that the Godly Yet is God's balance of telling the truth about sin and lifestyle YET refusing to let us go. Read Isaiah 30:18. Remember our lesson on cross-referencing from Week 1, Day 4? Try it again here. (In case you need some, I'll share mine. Try Psalm 34:8, Proverbs 16:20 and Jeremiah 17:7). Write down what you learn.

Back to Isaiah 30:18; do you see the Godly YET?

"For the Lord is a God of Justice" – *telling the truth about sin*

YET

"He longs to be gracious to you......show mercy to you." – *refusal to let go*

And somewhere in this process timed perfectly according to God's understanding of us, our lifetimes, our strengths, our weaknesses, and everything else we can't imagine is the Wait. For all of you who just rolled your eyes and want to give up, hang on. The Wait might be a time of structured discipline or just a season to perfect God's timing and we may hate it, but one thing is sure. What does God call those who wait for Him in the last sentence of Isaiah 30:18?

"Blessed" in Hebrew is called a particle of exclamation meaning that it is "an exclamatory interjection, usually associated with either great joy or great sorrow." [9] "Happy! is the man that findeth wisdom" (Proverbs 3:13), is an example of how you would write a particle of exclamation literally. I can't even tell you how much I love this. I see it as God's permission to use exclamation marks. I love them!! Warning, the next few paragraphs will be exclamatory! When I first started using text messages I'm sure that all my texts incited stress in the recipients because I use so many!!!!!! In texting, lots of !!! can elicit stress, like typing in ALL CAPS sounds like yelling. Something else about this particular word – blessed. The definition in the original Hebrew language means blessed. No big long deep explanation, just blessed. But here is something that will make you grin, I can hardly stand it. "This word is used only in the plural…"[10] Now why would God say it this way? The text is clear, mine says "blessed are ALL who wait on Him." God's point very clearly and literally is this, **"BLESSED! are ALL of you when you wait!"** In fact, He might even text it in all caps. We are blessed together along with Him as we wait and submit to His discipline and His timing. You are not alone as you wait and there are no exceptions to this promise. It may seem that your pew neighbor is getting more than her share of exclamatory blessing while you are continuing to just wait with lots of boring ………… and no !!!!!! His promise is that you will be blessed when you wait.

Brainstorm with me here, in your life who might be included in the plural blessedness of waiting? In other words, who are the people whose lives you most impact?

---

9   (Zodhiates), 2279
10   (Zodhiates), 2303

How might the lives of those toddlers, that man, that parent with Alzheimer's, that prodigal child, that vulgar co-worker, that special student that tries your last nerve, that........whoever be impacted if you started believing God to BLESS! you as you wait? Believe God for the blessing and believe Him for the companionship and believe Him for the exclamation mark. BLESSED! are you ALL when you wait.

My spell check is officially glad that this chapter is over – we barely survived.

Journal Prompt: You are with me as I wait for.....

Day 5: Pursuit

You know something I love about God? Only He can take a lesson that starts on grief and end with a blessing and an exclamation mark. What joy to study this and to know Him; now on to His love. Not only does God grieve but He also loves with pursuit and with discipline. Let's look together again at Hosea 2. Read verses 14-23 in several versions. After God pours out much of His anger and betrayal at the disobedience of His people He comes back to this amazing truth, His love pursues. His love pursues. Oh friend, His love pursues!

Thinking of this phrase, write down all the ways God's love pursued in Hosea 2:14-23.

I love this quote from my beloved ESV Study Bible notes, "the verb allure (2:14) can have the idea "to entice or seduce", but here it is paralleled with speak tenderly to her. The Lord will woo his estranged wife away from her lovers with the language of courtship."[11] This may seem weird to us, because many of us are religious people who like to keep God tidy and expected. It may seem awkward to those who are new to God's Word and just can't quite fathom a God who uses romance. Let me ask you, where do you think romance came from? Have you heard the term, "hopeless romantic?" God is this without the hopeless part. I take this phrase to mean someone who just can't be cured of a need for romance. No matter how many times it doesn't work or they get hurt, romance still rises up to the top of their reactions and temperament. God created that idea, but with Him there is always hope. He pursues His people and woos us with great intention and investment but never with

---

11   (ESV Study Bible), 1626

frivolity or flattery. He always tells us the truth about ourselves and about His love.

What do you notice about her reaction to God's tenderness in 2:15?

Some translations say answer or respond. I hope that you saw one other word – sing. God pursues you and speaks tenderly to you and turns your trouble into hope and gives you reason to sing and respond to Him. This Hosea passage is full of hope and tenderness and newness. Do you see the removal of all that would injure and the addition of new identity? Before we move on to a more difficult aspect of God's love, I want you to see God's provision of our needs.

Read Hosea 2:5 and 8. What are the things that the wayward one (us) needs in verse 5?

Note anything you learn in your study notes about the purpose of these items.

Who does she credit for them?

Who actually gives her the things she needs according to verse 8?

How does she use these items?

"Baal was the weather-god worshipped in Syria-Palestine who had control over agriculture and fertility, rainfall and productivity. Since Ancient Israel was always an agricultural society, Baal worship was of unrivaled importance."[12] Adult content warning – a large part of how the people in this area worshipped Baal was through temple prostitution. "This amounted to sexual intimacy at one of the pagan shrines, understood most probably as an act of imitative magic. That is, sexual behavior at these shrines was expected to cause the Baals to respond in like manner –to follow the worshippers by producing for them fertile seed and rain for a good crop..... When a worshipper selected a prostitute, he prayed, 'I beseech the goddess of Astarte to favor you and Baal to favor me.'"[13]

Can you see why this broke God's heart? He created these people. He had loved them and led them from captivity, endured their complaining and doubt as He brought them to a promised land, given them the kings they had begged for even though it meant rejection of Him, sent prophets to call them to right living and relationship with Him, and still they gave way to their fears. They were afraid that their wives would be barren or their crops would fail and so they pursued the solution that the world around them offered. Can you imagine an Israelite farmer, desperate to feed his family, exhausted by a faith that seems empty? He's unsure about what the God of his heritage really thinks about him because the priests he looked to for guidance were corrupt and self-seeking. In his

12   (ESV Study Bible), 1620.
13   (ESV Study Bible), 1620.

confusion he overhears this wild idea that another god could offer hope. It only makes sense, he needs a productive harvest and a large family, and that's what this god is all about. The solution appeals to his senses. It's worth the price to seek his favor, what does he have to lose? But the cost for his family and his soul is more than he ever expected to pay.

I would imagine that you must be ready to move on and that your stomach is as soured as mine since we've paused to consider this scenario. But first, I want you to consider something very interesting in the description of this false religion. Did you see that in this manner of worship the worshippers expected the Baal to "respond in like manner?" This is something that strikes home. If you haven't already felt the alarm of conviction bang in your chest, feel it now. Could it be that we choose idolatry because we think we can make our new god(s) follow us? Are we reluctant to follow God with everything we have because we can't manipulate Him? Every time I move ahead in my life, expecting God to move the way I want, calling back to Him, "Hey follow me!" I am choosing the way of Gomer. God will not follow me, He will not follow you. He loves us too much to allow us to boss Him.

What are some ways that you tell God to follow you?

After you have come clean about it, review Isaiah 30:18 and your cross-references from yesterday and find God's promise of blessing.

Journal Prompt: I see that I have been asking God to follow me as I.....

Week 3 – Redemption

Day 1: Discipline

Read Hosea 2:9-13 and see the loss. List them here:

Part of me wishes we could skip this part, but this is Gomer's choice, this is our choice when we walk away from Him, "but me she forgot" (verse 13). We can lose for a time the precious gift of His provision. Please see that this discipline came only when she refused to acknowledge Him. Only God knows this particular boundary. God understands the way that I struggle and He can handle my hard questions. He is not looking for a moment of weakness so He can pull the rug out from under my feet under the guise of discipline. BUT, and this is a big one, when I refuse Him as Gomer refused Hosea, I get exactly what I asked for – a lifestyle that doesn't include Him or His blessings. If you missed this go back and see how she flaunts her lifestyle apart from God. I'm not talking about your salvation here. I'm talking about the way God deals with us in everyday life. See this also: just as only God knows when we have made the decision to walk away from Him, He also knows when we are ready to come home. So don't let the expectations of others define this boundary for you, you can always come home. Read Matthew 11:28 and John 6:37 and record God's opinion on coming home.

The change between verses 13 (today's lesson) and 14 (yesterday's lesson) of Hosea chapter 2 is the miraculous capacity and blending of God's pursuing and disciplining love. Please don't get so stuck in the difficult imagery of loss in verses 9-13 that you miss God's true intention, which is to get us to verse 14 where another Godly Yet lives in the therefore. This may be new, but I believe God's discipline over us works best couched in a firm understanding of His love and redemption. If you are serious about following God with a pure heart your first step shouldn't be to seek cleansing, it should be to settle firmly and deeply into an immovable understanding of His great love for you; the cleansing of repentance will be quick to follow. You could no more hold it back than a tidal wave.

Read some more about how God disciplines in Hebrews 12:7-12. Focus on God's motivation. Why does He use discipline in your life?

Journal Prompt: God is teaching me discipline right now through......

Day 2: God's Hedge

Today we are going to study God's Hedge. You may have heard the church phrase "hedge of protection" especially in prayers. One of my favorite comedians teases church folks about using such phrases, articulating that our enemy may not be as afraid of greenery as our prayers reflect. We aren't going to debate the effectiveness of the hedge-praying deacon. Instead, we're going to do a compare and contrast of the hedge in Hosea and a hedge in the book of Job. Read Hosea 2:6 and describe the hedge that surrounded Gomer. The NIV calls the hedge "thorn bushes," read it in several versions noting what you learn. What is the purpose of the hedge?

Now read Job 1:10. Who is having this conversation? What is the purpose of the hedge?

You found that in Hosea the purpose of the hedge is a boundary. In Job the purpose of the hedge is protection. In Gomer's case God was trying to keep her home, setting the hedge to remind her of where she really found safety. In Job's case, the hedge was keeping an outside threat from claiming him and coming in.

Read Job 3:23, what does Job think the purpose of his hedge is all about?

What did we just read is the real purpose of Job's hedge? Are they on the same page, so to speak?

Now the Bible tells us that Job never denied God, but He complained a lot. I love the end of the book where God puts the complaining in check and all Job can do is hold his hand over his mouth – no kidding, it's in there! But that's for another study. So, consider your own life. Has God ever put a thorn bush or a hedge in your life? What was it?

Did you perceive it as protection or as a boundary?

Why is it that we kick our way through boundary hedges one day, while complaining that God isn't protecting us the next, refusing to see that outside the hedge is a loss of His protection? Maybe this is a good day for an attitude change about the hedges in your life. Perhaps what you've been complaining against as an obstacle in your life is really a protective boundary. Could today be the day to lay down the giant spiritual yard shears you are using against God's hedge and recognize the boundary and protection that are His gifts to you? I first saw the connection between Hosea and Job reading a commentary on the Minor Prophets by James Montgomery Boice. This is how he closes the section on the hedge.

"If you take the talents God has given you and then run away from him to seek whatever it is you want out of this life, God will first come gently to remind you that he is the source of the gifts you squandered and that you are doing wrong to squander them…..Do you think that God will not do this? That he is too "kind"? I tell you that God will do it. He is faithful to his nature and will not allow the one he loves to be destroyed through an adulterous infatuation with this world's idols."[14]

Journal Prompt: The hedge in my life is…..I can cooperate with God's protection by…..

---

14   (Boice), 27.

Day 3: Hazy Days of Awakening

Some scholars believe that the book of Hosea might've been a collection of many mini-sermons or oracles that Hosea delivered over the course of his ministry to Israel. If so it might explain why there are some crazy hard-to-follow disjointed parts of the book. We are going to jump ahead and look at two verses in the book where we can find explicitly stated one of God's themes, not just in Hosea, but throughout His Word. The concept is redemption. Maybe, like the hedge prayer, this is little more than a church word to you. Maybe you know this word and seeing it makes your heart flip because you know how precious it is. I love the line to an old hymn that says, "Redeeming Love has been my theme, and shall be 'til I die." I have it framed on the wall in my home. Although God is beyond capturing, I believe the reality of redeeming love most closely encapsulates His intention for us.

Remember Gomer? Where was she when we last saw her? If you don't remember, check Hosea 3:2 (Week 1, Day 2).

Read all 5 verses of Hosea 3. Gomer's abandonment of her family is assumed as God describes the painful idolatry of His people in chapter 2. Now God's instruction comes again to Hosea. What is he instructed to do in verse 1?

How much does it cost him?

The standard price for a slave was thirty shekels of silver, Gomer sold for half that amount. I wonder so much about the exact terms and circumstances of Gomer's bailout. Was she chained and offered on a sale block? Was she stripped and auctioned, humiliated that her value was so low? Did she look for Hosea across the crowd, both hoping and fearing he would come? Perhaps Hosea sought her out privately and brokered the deal with whoever now owned her. Did Hosea bargain fifteen shekels plus nine bushels of grain because that is all he had? The amount is all the detail we are given and it is low. Although we don't have Gomer's excuses or explanations I would imagine that this stop in her story was not part of her original plan. She trusted a lie to give her freedom and instead it enslaved her.

What lies have you believed that ultimately enslaved you?

Read Titus 3:3-8. There is a Godly YET in the beginning of verse 4. What appears and breaks the chains of slavery?

He saved us, half priced runaway slaves. According to Titus 3, He saves because He is mercy. He saves because we are heirs and that's how He always sees us. He saves and now we can be devoted to Him and to doing good. In verse 8 Paul tells Titus to "insist" on these things. What do you think he is talking about? What are the "these things"?

Please see that these things are not the good doings, they are the core beliefs in God's mercy and salvation and identity from verses

4-7. Good Doings always come from a good understanding of identity and the gratitude that follows mercy.

Meanwhile back in Hosea, Gomer has just been bought by her husband. Can you imagine that ride home? Maybe you've endured a similar paralyzing and painful awkwardness. There are no words to describe the condition of this marriage and this home in these moments. What do you think it might've been like?

As soon as they cross the welcome mat back into the home Gomer abandoned, what are Hosea's instructions in verse 3? What strikes you about this verse?

I get his instructions to her, yes she has to stop sleeping with other men. But why does he say "so will I also be to you"? He's been faithful; in fact he now owns her and many would say she owes him. The instruction here is very clear. Gomer is to come home and be reunited with her family, but she and Hosea are not to share the same bed. Maybe Hosea wisely knew that his wife would just shift her addictions from others toward him. Maybe he knew that she would give her body to him but only as she had to many others – for payment. What does 1 Corinthians 7:5 teach about the purpose of abstaining from marital intimacy for a season?

When we look at Hosea 3:4, we get a better understanding of why Hosea and Gomer are sharing a home ONLY for now. All the things listed in verse four are people and items that were designed to lead God's people to worship Him with purity, things that they twisted into an ugly betrayal of idol worship. The beautiful and pure act of intimacy in Gomer's marriage has been twisted into a painful betrayal. I love how the Message renders the end of verse five, "They'll come back chastened to reverence before God and his good gifts, ready for the End of the story of his love." These are the hazy days of chastening. The days for purification, where all the toxins Gomer has invited into her life can fade away while she is safe. The days that offer her the clarity and safety to look forward to right relationships. As Hosea loves her the way God loves His people her heart can safely come home.

What vulnerabilities might Gomer face at this point in her life?

What are some things God created that the world turns into a betrayal?

Have you ever had an experience of waking up from such an attachment?

The simplicity of redemption is that you were created by God to know and live in close relationship with Him. Because of sin you have sold yourself into slavery. God buys you back and nurses you through the painful detox until you are able to believe you are who He's always said you are and live that way.

Journal Prompt: I can cherish the days of chastening because.....

Day 4: The Call and Whistle of Redemption

Read Hosea 7:13, 13:14. The word redeem in both of these verses is the Hebrew word "padah." It means "to sever, to redeem by paying a price, to ransom, to set free, to let go, to dismiss, to rescue, to deliver from danger. The essential meaning is achieving the transfer of ownership from one to another through payment or by something of equivalent value."[15] We will be spending today and tomorrow defining redemption. What is your initial reaction to this definition? Rewrite the meaning of redeem in your own words.

Now read Isaiah 50:1-5. Find the word redeem. What does it say?

Read Isaiah 50:1-2 again, how would you describe God's tone and attitude?

I believe this passage teaches that God allows periods of self-inflicted separation from Him. In other words, He will let you walk away from Him for a season if you choose to, but those seasons do not change your identity as His child. How did you answer the question about God's tone in verses one and two? I think it's almost sarcastic. God is saying, "Can you prove to me that you no longer belong to me? Show me the papers proving I gave you up! Was I forced to sell you into slavery because I owed

---

15   (Zodhiates), 2353.

someone? NO, you sold yourself! And when I came to save you….you weren't waiting. When I called out to rescue you, you weren't listening. Where were you? Do you think I can't do it? Don't you remember the stories of how I delivered your ancestors from Eqypt? I dried up the sea with a word! Don't you know I can save you? Don't you know I want to?"

What must it be like for Him to pursue His people and call to them to buy them back from their sins, only to find their faith absent?

How does this fit with your life and your personal relationship with Him?

Now read Zechariah 10:8 and glean a precious response. This is how it should be when God calls. The ESV says God whistles for us, yours might say signal. My sister-in-law has one of those great whistles I envy. I've practiced by myself and it just turns into a slobber fest. Her kids can hear it from anywhere and they come running because they know it is mom calling. There is safety and instruction in that whistle, along with an expectation of obedience. Have you ever imagined God whistling for you? This should be on the Sunday School checklist of things all Christians should know! I love this image. When you find yourself reeling from a fall, self-inflicted or otherwise, take heart knowing that as you wait, God is blessing. Be careful to watch for His redemption and listen for the whistle. Before we finish with this idea read a few verses down, Zechariah 10:12 and write out the promise of redemption.

Be strong in the Lord and walk in His name.

Journal Prompt: Picturing God whistling for me makes me…..

Day 5: Walking Redeemed

I pray that you are convinced to follow God's redemptive call, to heed the whistle. This day's lesson finds us a few days into the redemption detox. The haze is lifting and we are feeling the familiarity of home. So let's talk about what it means to walk in redemption. In other words, how do we stay on the right track? Read Isaiah 35 several times in your favorite translations. What do you learn about redemption?

Focus on verses 8-10 for a minute. I love the ESV in verse eight where it says, "even if they are fools, they shall not go astray." God has just introduced the path the redeemed are to walk. It's a brand new highway called "The Way of Holiness." It's completely safe, the best road trip ever and by the way you can't get lost here. If you were in my Wednesday morning Bible Study, this is where I would get all mushy and barely able to keep my composure because it makes me feel loved that God foresees and reassures me even in all my foolishness.

Before we move on, specifically describe the people walking on this highway.

Although you can find Jesus all through the Old Testament, we get to actually see His life in the New Testament. As you might imagine, His life and sacrifice make all the difference when it comes to redemption! Remember yesterday we learned that to be redeemed means that I am rescued, ransomed and someone has to pay.

What do these verses teach about redemption?
Matthew 20:28

1 Peter 1:18-19

Now read 1 Peter 2:21-25. This passage paints a beautiful all-encompassing picture of redemption. What did your redemption cost?
Romans 3:22-24

Titus 2:11-14

Ephesians 1:7-8

This is a very important point about the biblical concept of redemption. It is never without cost. Jesus is your redemption. He is mine. He lived and died and lives again to make a way for us to be rescued from slavery. I hope you could see this clearly in the verses you studied. We are told in Titus that this truth empowers us to live differently – to be zealous to do good. We are told in 1 Peter to return to Him, the "Shepherd and Guardian of our souls". Truly God is our only safe place. The cost to redeem you was much greater than fifteen shekels. There is no cost too high, even the life of His Son.

Close where you started. Read anew Hosea 7:3 and 13:14. In light of everything you've learned so far, what does it mean for God to redeem you?

Journal Prompt: Jesus redeemed me, I am.....

Week 4 – The Case Against God's People

Day 1: Spiritual Amnesia and the Kids

With the beginning of Hosea four we are launching into a prophetic lawsuit. God gives us a courtroom scene so we can understand what He's calling His people out of. This type of literary device was also used by some of Hosea's contemporaries (see Isaiah 3:13-15 and Micah 6:2). It's also called a controversy. You can see the word in Hosea 4:1, "The Lord has a **controversy** with the inhabitants of the land." This word is the opposite of quietness which should have been the strength of God's people (Isaiah 30:15).

Imagine that you are sitting in a courtroom watching this unfold. Hosea is the prosecuting attorney and God's people are the defendants. Hosea opens God's case against His people with some serious stuff. Read Hosea 4:1-3 and note the major points in Hosea's argument. What are God's complaints against the people?

The way I see it there are two major problems; spiritual amnesia and generational idolatry. Let's talk about these things and see how scarily similar they are to mistakes we make every day.

Spiritual Amnesia (4:1): They forgot God by letting these three things go missing in their relationship with Him:

1. Faithfulness – TRUTH. Literally this means stability or firmness. When they quit being careful about Truth they lost their ability to be faithful. They also lost their security when they gave up their faithfulness to God.

2. Steadfast Love – MERCY. They forgot how to receive or give God's love. We learn in 1 John 4:19 that "we love because He first loved us." We love well as a reflection of our accurate understanding of His love for us. The next time you begin to think that you are doing ok loving your loved ones on your own without staying closely attached to God, you are being deceived. We don't do this on purpose, but we still do it all the time.

Can you think of some ways you prioritize loving others over an accurate understanding of God's love for you?

3. Knowledge of God. They let go of understanding or interacting with Him and His Word. His expectations and promises no longer were a part of their daily lives. They became religious and forgot the wonder He had been to them and to their ancestors personally.

How about you? How much do you interact with God in your daily life?

In case you've not been warned about this, being religious is not godly. It's as dangerous as being rebellious. We'll talk about this some more in Week 6, but if this hits you brand new today don't go any further without taking it to God. He is delighted to transform religion into real vibrant relationship.

Much of the rest of the book of Hosea hinges on understanding these problems and overcoming them. Which one of the above numbered issues is the hardest for you to hold onto and remember? Why?

This is a mid-day journaling session. Before you move on to the second half of today's study read carefully and prayerfully Psalm 139:23-24. Then spend some time in prayer considering the three specific areas we covered today, asking God to show you where you need strength and where you need to make corrections. Maybe you need to spend some time patching your hedge today. Put it in writing in your journal along with a specific correction plan. After you've written a plan, share it with someone who can help hold you accountable.

Generational Idolatry: This is the second complaint Hosea brings against the people on God's behalf. Read Hosea 4:4-9. What is the basis of God's complaint?

Think back to what we already have studied about idolatry. Redefine idolatry:

Now add in the kids. If you don't have children you aren't off the hook, because there is a younger generation all around watching the way you live, being impacted by the lies or the truth you teach with your words and actions and attachments.

Read Judges 2:10 and compare it with Psalm 78:5-8. What do you learn? What is our responsibility to the next generation?

If there comes a generation behind us that doesn't know God or the wonders He has done, then shame on us. I'm not a big fan of that phrase, but it is appropriate here. Please hear me, I'm not talking about a prodigal child who knows the truth and is living in his own "Gomer-land." God is waiting and whistling for him as we speak. These passages refer to our lazy disregard of God's command to tell children about Him. It is our fault if they don't know! According to Psalm 78 we are to teach them God's truths so that they will set their hope in God, allowing themselves to be surrounded by His truth and love, being faithful to His ways, not forgetting His works and keeping His commandments.

Last summer my oldest daughter was planning to go on her first mission trip with her dad. We found out late that her passport was going to expire just before she went. Even with the extra effort and expense to expedite the return of her passport, it looked very much like it wouldn't come in time. The members of the mission team had been meeting together and planning and knew about this particular kink in the plans. One of the men on the team sent our daughter a letter full of truth reminding her to trust God in the midst of the uncertainty. She decided to do just that, and shared her lesson with others who affirmed her faith even more. The passport came and she was able to go and had a wonderful experience. But the best lesson of that trip was learned before she ever left home. She has adults in her life who care enough to tell her the truth about God, and she learned He is wondrous.

I know that this is not easy and doesn't look like what I just described on a day to day basis. I have a teenager, a tweener, and a preschooler at my house right now. There is almost always someone in a "rough stage," as moms like me describe it, with a fake smile and gritted teeth. There are days we can't get on to the good stuff of God's goodness because we just honestly can't make it past the mundane lessons of hygiene and nutrition (brush your teeth, eat your broccoli). If you feel caught there, take heart. The result of sharing Jesus with the children in our generation isn't here yet – it's the *result* and they don't typically show up until the end. We may get to view the results of our efforts as our children become adults sharing with the children of their generation, but mostly we just obey day by day and trust the results to Him. We send the letters of encouragement and teach the Sunday School lessons and cook the meals at camp and look for the invisible ones who don't have any Truth-tellers at home.

Go back to the list of things the Israelites were missing. Faithfulness, love, and knowledge of God (Truth, Mercy, the Word) are the weapons during these days on the battleground for my kids and their generation. Instead of being focused on how my kids are turning out, I should be evaluating more seriously how I parent them. How important is faithfulness – truth telling and teaching in our home? How much do we practice God-sized love and forgiveness in our family? How intentional are we to know our Creator? Those are the questions to ask and the plans to make.

What are some things you can do to make sharing God's light in the younger generation a bigger priority? Get specific, get a partner and a plan and get going.

Journal Prompt: I can be a better example for the next generation by.....

Day 2: Research for the Prosecution

You are a team working for the Prosecution. For today, you are working for Hosea. On trial are God's People. In the passages before you is all the evidence you need to convict them. It's your job to read these chapters and list the offenses against the Lord committed by His people. Be careful not to list the judgments against them, that's for the Judge (and we won't know what He decides until next week). <u>Only list what they've done wrong, according to God</u>. Read these passages and list only the offenses that they have committed.

Hosea 4

Hosea 5

Hosea 6

Now if you have time, choose some of the verses in these chapters and look up the cross-references. If you get stuck read them in other versions. Where did they go wrong? You might try charting their offenses using the three categories under Spiritual Amnesia from yesterday's lesson. The goal is for you to become well-acquainted with their mistakes.

Journal Prompt: These people make me feel…..

Day 3: Following Bad Leadership

Now that you have a bit more familiarity with the evidence against God's people, let's look more specifically at the biggies. Imagine Hosea setting these items on the edge of the jury box as he lays out the evidence of Israel's disobedience.

Item 1: *Willingness to Follow Bad Leadership*. This was scandalous. Hosea is accusing the preacher, for heaven's sake! Read Hosea 4:7-9 and 7:3. It's chilling. What do you see in the lives of Israel's leaders?

I remember reading a passage in 1 or 2 Kings years ago and seeing this pattern for the first time. I was so grieved to see line after line of names of Israel and Judah's kings following the same pattern. King So and So ruled some certain number of short years. He did evil in the sight of the Lord, and did not depart from the sins of his father. This had been the pattern for generations. Your cross-references will point you toward other prophets with this same message if you'd like to dig in a little deeper here. The corruption in the priesthood was rampant and extremely destructive.

Verse 9 says, "Like people, Like Priest." What do you think this statement means?

Have you seen this happen in modern church culture?

If you are in a position of leadership, please don't take it lightly. We all have influence that should be wielded carefully as the gift it is. Read 4:14 and describe the legacy of these leaders.

According to Hosea 5:1, the leaders of Israel were setting traps for the Israelite people instead of leading them to love and serve God. Although some of these men were intentionally cunning and wicked, we aren't told that all of them set out to lead their entire country away from God. What might've happened to them? How did they come to a place where they believed the lies of their surroundings instead of the one true God?

What about you? Have you ever sacrificed your influence?

I remember learning about this influence for the very first time. I was a young pastor's wife with two little kids. Our entire family had been working in the yard all day one weekend. We were hot, sweaty, dirty, and hungry so we ran to our local Taco Bell for dinner. While we were there, we saw a young married couple that had been visiting our church. Remember, my husband was their pastor. When we walked in and saw them and said hello they immediately got really weird and awkward. After a few stilted exchanges the young woman said, "Sooooo, you guys eat at Taco Bell?" I blinked profusely and bit one side of my lip so as not to blurt out something stupid. Instead I said, "Yes. We love Taco Bell." She said, "I guess I pictured you making gourmet meals all the time." Months later as we laughed about the awkwardness of our Taco Bell encounter, I realized that she had been teasing me just a little bit. At the time I was incredulous, tickled, and mortified. If there is anything about me that is communicating to others that I am above them and not right in the middle of them, something is horribly wrong. It's a lesson I never forgot.

Who follows you?

Read 1 Timothy 4:12. What are the five areas in which we are to set a good example?
1.

2.

3.

4.

5.

Give yourself a grade for each of these areas. Where do you need to improve?

Journal Prompt: I see that my influence is…..

Day 4: The Gift of Fleeting Repentance

Item 2: *Gift of Fleeting Repentance.* The second key piece of evidence that Hosea lays before the court is fake repentance. Have you ever received a fake apology? God doesn't appreciate it any more than you do. My kids still try to get away with this one – it may be the end of the fight, but there is no heart change. That's what the Israelites were after. They didn't want to fight with God; they wanted to be off the hook. But they weren't willing to change their hearts or their lives. Read the following verses, noting what you learn about their religious efforts.

Amos 5:21-24

Isaiah 1:11-17

Psalm 51:16-17

Hosea 6:6

The teaching of repentance is not a popular one today, but it is so very important. We'll be spending much of our last session on the topic, but it's appropriate that we also hit it briefly now. How would you define repentance and why should it be important to you?

Why do you think our genuine heartfelt repentance matters so much to Him? HINT, God is more interested in relationship than religion.

Read Hosea 6:1-6, 7:14-16, and 8:2 and try to figure out what made their confession shallow. Write down your ideas.

Consider the word "desire" in Hosea 6:6. According to the passage, what does God desire?

This word means "to like very much, to bend toward."[16] Think about what/who you really like, those people and things that inspire you to bend toward them. Are you grinning? That's how God feels about sincere repentance, about steady love. If you are hesitant to believe that God really wants to forgive you when you mess up, see this picture. As you try to work up the courage to offer an apology He is already leaning toward you grinning – He is delighted. Read the following verses in several translations and note in your journal what they teach.

1 John 1:8-9

Romans 10:9-10

---

16   (Zodhiates), 2317.

So, what does repentance look like and what does it require? Skip ahead to Hosea 14:1-4 and learn a bit more about God's intent for repentance. Oh, what a blessing to see the end of the story! We will be studying it in depth in our last session together, just thought you might like a glimpse.

Journal Prompt: Repentance is difficult for me because.....

Day 5: Refusal to Acknowledge God

Item 3: *Refusal to Acknowledge God.* Here is the third key piece of evidence, and it's condemning.

In Hosea 8:2-3, 14 God talks about His people's inability to effectively remember Him. Read these verses from Hosea to remember what God's trying to help them see. This is what we might call a recurring theme – and not just in Hosea, but all through the Old Testament.

None of us like to be ignored. It's a sad thing to feel invisible. But God is not vain, He doesn't want to be remembered so that we can just say a quick *"Hello There! I see you!"* He knows that left on our own, we are lost – quick to sell ourselves into slavery out of desperation or rebellion. Just like Gomer, we will run headlong into a thorn bush. He knows that remembering Him is life or death for us. The Israelites were originally taught how to remember God by Moses. Read the following verses and write out God's instructions to them.

Deuteronomy 4:23

Deuteronomy 6:10-12

Deuteronomy 8:10-14 and 19-20

In Deuteronomy 8:14, 19-20 God tells them what the outcome will be if they forget Him. What is it?

Remembering God should be a spiritual discipline in your life. It seems that you love Him enough that you just will, but you don't. Remember all the cute things that your kids said when they were little that you swore you would remember? Did you? I do better now because I blog about them, and that is exactly my point. Loving someone doesn't necessarily mean you'll remember them the way you should. Especially in our relationship with God, this level of remembrance comes from rehearsing and memorizing and practicing. Don't be lulled into believing that you can follow God without the discipline of intentional remembering. What do you spend your brain energy rehearsing? I remember once, as a newlywed, trying to engage my husband in conversation as we were driving. I asked that question all men love, "What are you thinking about?" To which he replied, "Nothing." I asked him about a thousand questions and realized that truly, he was thinking about nothing. We don't work that way. I can't remember a single time that my brain clicked to something from nothing. What about you? What do you spend most of your brain power thinking about? What are the recurrent themes?

To close this study from Deuteronomy, try re-writing the list you made of God's instructions for remembering into a plan for your own life, all to ensure you remember God.

Journal Prompt: Realizing times I forget God makes me feel…..

Week 5 – Coming Home

Day 1: Unflattering Pictures and the Whirlwind

After, or in the process of laying out the major pieces of evidence against God's people, Hosea throws in a few more examples to help them visualize what their behavior looks like to God. Read each of the following sections of verses and describe the picture He gives.

- 7:6-7

- 7:8-10

- 7:11-12

- 7:16

After you've looked them up, see which of these descriptions fits the point He's trying to make for each one.

1. Dangerous.
2. Pretty on one side, but unaware of ugliness on the other.
3. Ruled by smoldering desires easily fanned into full flame.
4. Senseless, going to the wrong places for help.

It's amazing how unflattering these descriptions are! I don't want my life to be characterized by any of these. How about you? Let's be quick to remember God and quick to repent when we've done wrong, so we don't find ourselves caught up in one of these very bad spiritual pictures.

For the most part, the sentencing is coming down in the next chapter, but we do get a little glimpse or hint of judgment or warning in Hosea 8:7. When compared to Hosea 10:12 our choice is clear.

Read Hosea 8:7 and Hosea 10:12. From each verse note what seed is planted and what grows from that seed.

What does it mean to sow the wind? Brainstorm and make a list of things that you might plant or allow someone else to plant in your life that would be considered "windy" or "empty". This is a great example of symbolism in Hosea. These pictures will really stick with us if we let our minds see them! Describe or draw it below.

Now consider the opposite of sowing the wind; sowing righteousness. What is the result of planting righteousness in your life?

Read Philippians 3:7-10 and note what you learn about righteousness.

You are righteous in God's eyes, but not because of anything you have done. Righteousness is a gift and while it comes to you with no strings attached; it wasn't free. Jesus already owned righteousness with God because He earned it. And then He paid for ours too. Recognition of this fact is what is blowing Paul's mind when he says, "I want to know Christ!" Keep this in mind and answer this question; how can you sow righteousness in your life?

Read this quote and then journal your response to it; "Do you think this does not happen? I tell you it does happen even in the most evangelical churches. There are people who could be very useful in the Lord's work but who are useless simply because they are taken up with their jobs, families, cars, or house. They have no time for service. Others are made useless by sin. They have forgotten God by the way they are living, wrongly thinking that they can profess Jesus as Savior while ignoring Him as Lord......Is it not true that in such churches we are sowing the seed of the neglect of God and will reap the whirlwind?"
James Montgomery Boice, The Minor Prophets, Volume 1, page 65.

Journal Prompt: My reaction to the quote by James Boice.....

Day 2: The Sentencing

This may be the most difficult part of the study of Hosea – the sentence. Israel forgot God and ignored His loving and stern warnings to return to the safety of relationship with Him. Glance back over the last session. What sentence would you have chosen for them? We probably would've let them off easy, after all, we can relate to them. God can never be less than He is, and He is Holy. The lifestyle they had chosen as a nation was not acceptable for God's people. The sentence He hands down although just, is harsh in our eyes and so blinds us toward God's compassion. As you wade through the loss that Israel faces, keep two things in mind. First, these losses are the results of their own sinful choices. They are a glimpse of consequences apart from God's mercy. Second, these losses are NOT the end of the story. Allow yourself to sink into the depth of these losses. Understand that the risk of walking away from Him is not worth any imagined freedom. Don't be afraid to try to understand God in this sentencing, remembering that Hope is just around the corner. In the Godly Yet, this day's study is about God's commitment to always telling us the truth about our lives and our sin.

Because they forgot Him and persisted in a life of sin, the Israelites lose certain privileges. Imagine hearing these losses read out as a jury foreman would read a guilty verdict in a courtroom. Over the course of Hosea Chapter 8, 9, 10 as well as 12 and 13, I see these eight privileges lost for the season of their rebellion. You can read these chapters through or follow the passages I have pulled out for you. This is an ideal place to read from different translations.

Read the passages listed underneath each privilege and <u>summarize what is lost</u>. Then, go back and <u>note any significance</u> you see.
- The Loss of the Privilege of God's Favor
  - 9:15,17
  - Jeremiah 6:27-30
  - 7:13

- The Loss of the Privilege of Understanding His Word
  - 8:12
  - 9:7-9
  - Matthew 13:14-16

- The Loss of the Privilege of Worship
  - 10:2b, 5-8
  - 13:2

- The Loss of the Privilege of Civil Peace
  - 10:3-4
  - 13:9-10
  - Isaiah 48:18

- The Loss of the Privilege of Material Security
  - 10:13-15
  - 9:17
  - 12:9

- The Loss of the Privilege of Physical Fruitfulness
  - 9:10-17
  - 10:1-2

- The Loss of the Privilege of Protection
  - 13:4-9

- The Loss of the Privilege of GRACE
  - 10:2
  - 12:14
  - 13:16

This is why there aren't many Bible Studies on Hosea. We can't take it. The first time I taught this I felt sick. I looked out on the faces of the precious women in my Bible Study and just so sincerely wanted to skip this part. I fretted that I would misrepresent God's intention in these verses and plant a seed of bitterness in one of their lives. As we talked, I just kept praying for clarity and endurance to see it through. I said several times in that lesson, "just stick with me – hang on!" We live in an age where we take God's grace and Jesus' sacrifice for granted and considering these losses in the wake of idolatry is a journey we are not typically willing to make. If you feel angry, sick, depressed, or guilty that's OK, "just stick with me – hang on!"

Do you see how these losses build on one another? We think we can live without the privilege of God's favor or the privilege of worship, ignoring opportunities to please Him and spend time with Him. But when we begin to lose the privilege of material security or physical fruitfulness we assume God is not who we've believed Him to be in the past; that we've been fooled and He isn't as faithful as we thought. We live and are raising children in a culture that tolerates almost all kinds of worldviews except a Biblical one. People can't pick and choose privileges and losses as God's children. We cannot ignore Him in our daily life and then scorn the consequences He allows into our lives when things go the way we directed them but not the way we expected.

If God were to hold one of those losses against you, what would it be? Which would be the hardest for you?

Can you think of any verses that reassure you that He doesn't work that way? Try Psalm 103.

What have you learned about keeping your relationship with God healthy so that you don't have to face such consequences?

How does what you've already studied in Hosea help you to interpret and apply this lesson?

If you feel stuck here, please go back and review the lessons on redemption. We may want to kick and scream and rail that God would take these things from His people. But, HEAR this! These difficult chapters are God's commitment to your redemption and mine. The glimpse into the real lives of these Israelites angers and wounds me and causes me to feel fear toward Him *if* I don't understand His redeeming love. God meets that fear with the other side of the Godly YET, but first we have to walk through these days of loss.

Journal Prompt: This emotional lesson reminds me that.....

Day 3: Coming Home, Our Part

In the midst of these verses full of tragic consequences, God's great love for His people shows up as it always does. Read Hosea 10:12 and 12:6. I've divided the truth from these verses into two sections; a list of our responsibility in the Godly Yet and God's Responsibility in the Godly Yet.

Look at both verses and list the things we are to do.

Hopefully your list looks like mine. This is what I found. We are to:

Sow righteousness – Righteousness is just a fancy way of saying "to be right with." Remember what we reap when we sow righteousness in Chapter 8? What was it?

We need to be intentional about staying right with God. Ultimately my righteousness depends completely on what Jesus has done for my salvation. BUT, I need to be sensitive to staying closely connected to God, reaping the promise of His love. How do you do that in your life?

Break up unplowed ground – You know that part of your life that you just leave alone because you are afraid you can't deal with it? That part that if you scratch the surface it might erupt in a way you can't control? It's time to deal with it. The secret fears and insecurities and hidden sins stand in the way of your redemption. Most of us don't hide this as well as we think. When my little sister was a toddler, she got into a plate of peanut butter topped graham crackers. My dad asked her about it and she lied, cutely. When he pushed her a little bit more she told him that she did NOT eat the crackers, he could just ask Jesus when He got to heaven! The peanut butter was all over her face, spread from chin to nose to forehead where she had licked the cracker. The certainty of her innocence was sincere, but wrong. Could it be that God is trying to get your attention, convince you of a place you think you've hidden but really it's all over your life? Let the security of God's great and unchanging love for you be your "plow" and get after it.

Seek the Lord
Return
I imagine these two working together. To seek the Lord means you keep your eyes on Him. To return to Him means you follow Him, even if it is moving from a place of rebellion to a place of obedience. Read 2 Timothy 3:16 and write out the four benefits of God's Word. Circle the one that you think most closely represents the instruction to return.

1.

2.

3.

4.

I love to teach this passage. If we were together this would include a visual lesson with us walking down a path with God; complete with detours and a return, probably some hops, clapping, and fist bumps too. I love that God is so complete in the way He instructs us through His Word; not controlling, but very complete. Most religions and other gods just try to convince us of where we are wrong offering no power to change or return. Only our God, living and active and mighty to save gives teaching that instructs first, then convinces us we are wrong when we are veering off the path. He never leaves us there to figure things out on our own. He corrects us, showing us the way home and continues to give us the training that we need to keep following Him. Even in this passage in 2 Timothy there is the Godly Yet.

If you have unplowed ground, you know exactly where it is. If you've breezed through this lesson, take a few minutes and ask God what He thinks and then listen, receive correction and be willing to follow Him home.

Journal Prompt: I can get started plowing in my life by......

Day 4: Coming Home – Our Part

From yesterday, review the first 4 steps we are to take on our journey toward home:

1.

2.

3.

4.

Now for two more; we are also to:

Maintain Love and Justice

This is all about reflecting the Godly Yet in your own life. How can you balance the "truth-telling never let you go – ness" of God in your relationships?

Read John 15:12. How are we to love one another?

It's imperative that we strive to maintain love, that we prioritize loving others the way Jesus loves us. Start this intentionally today, beginning with the people who live under your roof and branch out from there.

Read 2 Chronicles 9:7-9. This is a tribute given by the Queen of Sheba when she visits King Solomon. Note that this is not a woman of God, this is a visitor in God's land coming to observe God's people and their ruler. What does she say about Solomon and the people? What does she say about God?

I think it's amazing that she could understand this much about God's heart for His people and His expectations of them. Look at exactly what she says God expects for Solomon to lead the people to do at the end of verse 8 and see if it sounds familiar.

Love and justice were created by God to work together. This is God's way of telling us to follow Him in translating the Godly Yet into our relationships. All through the Scripture He instructs His people to care for one another. Here are two pairs of Scripture showing God's actions and how we are to mimic them. What do you see?

Psalm 68:5 (God) and Isaiah 1:17 (Us)

Psalm 99:8 (God) and Ephesians 4:32 (Us)

Describe both extremes of a relationship that is heavy on either end of this dynamic duo.

Too heavy on Justice:

Too heavy on Love:

You don't need to wonder if you need to be practicing the Godly Yet, you do. There are people all around that desperately need to see a truthful balanced representation of God's character. When we only focus on telling the truth of God, we alienate those He desperately wants to join His family. When we only focus on accepting people who dishonor and discredit Him, we skew the power of His character and mislead those who desperately need to find Him. We must follow God day by day, seeking His example of tender and tough truth telling.

Now on to the last item on our list of things to do to Come Home.

Wait

Look at the depth of this word in Hebrew. It means "to bind together (by twisting); to collect; to be gathered together ; to be joined, to meet, to lie in wait for someone; to expect, await, look for patiently, hope; to be confident, trust; to be enduring."[17]

We think of waiting as a negative thing. I dislike waiting- a lot. Is this a correct view of waiting according to the definition above?

Without a doubt waiting is a spiritual discipline that is intentional. God does it on purpose and for a purpose. Waiting makes me squirm because it makes me feel forgotten and powerless. Read the following verses and record what you learn about waiting.

Psalm 27:13-14

Psalm 40:1-3

---

17   (Zodhiates), 2361.

Now answer these questions. What should you be doing while you wait?

What is at least one important purpose of waiting according to Psalm 40:3?

Sometimes one of the purposes of waiting is for God to work a redeeming reversal for all to see. Read Psalm 147:10-14. I want to address a specific part of the losses we studied earlier (Day 2), the loss of physical fruitfulness. The people God loved made decisions including child sacrifice that stole from their gift to have babies. Psalm 147:13 says that God "blesses your children within you." This Psalm is a praise song written to celebrate the "building up of Jerusalem" as God "gathers the outcasts of Israel." (verse 2). Are you connecting the dots yet? Because of their devastating choices, even the precious gift to bear children is lost to many of them for a time, but God never lets Satan sing the last verse. These verses in Psalm 147 are the reversal of the losses that the people experience in the time of Hosea, which was His goal all along.

Journal Prompt: The hardest step for me to take coming home is…..

Day 5: Welcomed Home

Before we move on to God's Part in our homecoming we are going to go on a Biblical Scavenger Hunt. I'll just confess up front, this is more on waiting. You know we need it! Different Hebrew words for "wait" are in each of these verses, BUT they aren't always translated "wait". Read the following verses and see if you can find the "waits". You will need to check different translations. Make a list of all the English words you find that are used for "wait".

- Psalm 25:5,21

- Psalm 33:20-22

- Psalm 37:7, 34

- Psalm 39:7

- Psalm 119:43, 74, 81, 114, 147

- Psalm 130

- Psalm 147:10-14

- Isaiah 33:2

- Isaiah 40:31

Choose your favorite verse from the above list and write it into a prayer. Memorize it, and soak in it for the rest of the day. Let it become part of your heart so that when waiting becomes challenging for you this verse will be there to strengthen and comfort you.

Now let's talk about ***God's Responsibility***. Returning to Hosea 10:12 and 12:6, make a list this time of God's responsibility.

Here's what I see. God does:

- Produce fruit and offer unfailing love.
- Come to us.
- Shower us with Righteousness.

Our list may be longer than God's, but who has the most difficult part? We plow up the hard spots in our lives and plant the seeds and God makes the fruit grow. We come home and seek Him and wait and He shows up and showers His righteousness on us. God doesn't have to practice these things like we do. He is them. He does them. Do you see the miraculous nature of healing? God does these things that we could never do for ourselves.

Read Isaiah 26:8 and write it here:

We live up to our end only by remembering Him and His abilities. By the way, I have to throw a word study in here. The Hebrew word for "shower" means to pour out with controlled aim[18]. God isn't stingy and He isn't accidental when He pours out His blessing. He's aiming for YOU! Read Isaiah 26:8 and John 15:5 and write out anew how you can acknowledge God's amazing healing power and what you need to do to flourish under His protective plan for your life.

---

18   (Zodhiates), 2323.

Read Hosea 10:12 and 12:6 and then reconsider our list:
- Sow righteousness

- Break up unplowed ground

- Seek the Lord

- Return

- Maintain Love and Justice

- Wait

Today I want you to define what it means for you right now where you are to practice each of these things. Next to each one listed above write the steps you can take to practice these disciplines. Take your time and really consider these things. For this to be a beneficial exercise, you must imagine them happening in your real life. The key word is PRACTICE. These are things that need to become daily disciplines in our life.

Journal Prompt: My responsibility in finding healing from the broken spots in my relationship with God is......

Week 6 – Walk on with Repentance on Your Mind

Day 1: Past Remembered – Father

In the midst of the chapter where God is laying out His case against His people, His attachment to them overwhelms Him and He begins to remember earlier days when His people loved Him and listened to Him.

Read Hosea 11:1-4. This is God as Father remembering His past with His people. Here He identifies Himself as a personal, attentive and nurturing Father. The concept of God being our Father is familiar to many of us. But this would have been quite a new concept to those listening to this for the first time. Have you ever helped a baby try to walk? You lean over him, both of you facing the same direction. You hold his hands, while his arms are raised up over his head and he walks while you keep him steady. I imagine this as God's idea in Hosea 11:3-4. Read the following verses and then describe yourself as God sees you, be specific.

- Hosea 11:1-4

- Romans 8:15

- Galatians 4:6

Now read Hosea 11:5-7 where God reminds them of their present situation. This is the reality of impending judgment. After you read these verses, summarize the situation the Israelites are facing in one word and write it here:

"The relationship between God and his chosen must not be viewed as a formality. These emotional outpourings demonstrate that the Lord is a person, filled with compassion--unlike the lifeless Baals. His affection weighs heavier than Israel's ingratitude, and He cannot bring himself to renounce his people even though they renounce him."[19]

Faithful to the Godly Yet, God doesn't leave them in their present situation. Although there will still be consequences to pay, God assures them that their future is with Him. Read Hosea 11:8-11 and just let the gentleness wave over you. At the end of verse 8 in my version God says, "my heart recoils within me; my compassion grows warm and tender." What causes this type of reaction? Have you ever experienced something like this? If so, describe the circumstances.

One summer off from college I was working away from home and my parents came to see me after a devastating break up from my college boyfriend. My dad lay on my bed while I paced and bounced and raged, it couldn't have been easy for him. He could've said I told you so, but he just listened steadily and calmly. This picture of our Heavenly Father from verse 8 could've been an exact description. I could see the warmth and tenderness on his face. The impact that this interaction with my dad had on my life was transforming although I didn't recognize it until almost two years later as my future husband and I walked into a restaurant where he would meet my parents for the first time. My very confident Todd – the epitome of "the parents are gonna love him" got all weird and stopped dead in his tracks. I turned and looked at him and asked what he was waiting for. I wanted to say, "Steak....Dr. Pepper....Inside." He said, "What if your dad doesn't like me? From what you've said about him, he's gotta like me." Because of my previous experience and my dad's tender reaction to my mistakes that

19   (ESV Study Bible) 1638.

night I had become convinced that I should never date anyone without my dad's approval ever again. I hadn't realized how clearly I had communicated this. It was just a part of me. I had learned how prone I was to make mistakes and that I could trust my Father's judgment. Are you following? In the way that you live is your desperation to follow God so strongly communicated that everything else says, "Her dad's gotta like me if I'm to remain a part of her life?"

Read Jeremiah 31:20. Rewrite it as if you are receiving it. For example, start like this: "Am I not God's dear daughter?......."

I hope that right now you see the choice you have. Because of your present reality, full of whatever things threaten to keep you from Him, you may not see the truth of your future as God's child. It may not be a looming consequence of rebellion like the Israelites faced. Perhaps the greatest threat for your spiritual life right now is mundane ease. Could it be fear or selfishness or a need for retribution or refusal to forgive?

What are the things in your present reality that keep you from Him?

Go back and read your paraphrase of Jeremiah 31:20 with the present reality you just listed in mind. God does not leave you here alone although He might require that you walk through the difficulty of it with Him by your side. He knows that your future is secure, even when you refuse to believe it. He knows that what is real to you now doesn't even compare to the reality He has prepared for you. He waits and longs for you as you learn. The fact that you are reading these words and studying something as difficult as the Book of Hosea shows that you are making an effort to know Him and He will honor it. Treasure and trust Him as Faithful Father the same way He cherishes you as Precious Daughter.

Journal Prompt: In my present reality I fear.....

Day 2: Undone – Present Reality

Psalm 106 is an amazing summary of the history of God's people. As you read all 48 verses make note of the patterns you notice. Take some time with this, I promise it's worth it.

Now go back over the Psalm and note specifically God's intervention in the events listed.

Hopefully now you have two lists – one of the people's activities and one of God's intervention. How would you describe each of them?

Many of the phrases in this passage make me so sad, but none more than verse 24. It says "they despised the pleasant land, having no faith in His promise." Part of the definition for the word despised means to "feel undone."[20] I think we struggle to believe God's promises sometimes because we just feel unraveled. This isn't a deliberate shunning of God's pleasant land; it's just a focus on the overwhelming tasks or pain in our present reality. Could it be that when I choose to sink into my undone emotions I am despising the pleasant land God has given me?

What makes you feel undone?

How might these be a rejection of God's promises?

I feel undone all the time. Have you ever said, "I've had it up to here!" Being overwhelmed is a very common struggle for women. Our expectations of ourselves are often too high and unreasonable and off-target. Our schedules get interrupted and our plans don't work the way we'd imagined. Disappointment turns into lethargy and the tasks and expectations pile up, making us feel like a failure and completely overwhelmed. Seriously, I'm tired just typing up that paragraph - it's so revolving door familiar.

Review your list of the patterns of the Israelites in Psalm 106. Can you find any common ground? What do you think might've made them feel undone?

---

20   (Zodhiates), 2329.

Did God intervene from a distance or right in the middle of their mess? Don't let the honesty of His reactions trip you up. These reactions stem from an undeniable love for them as well as frustration when they seem resolved to stay down, even though He has called them to a higher place.

Read Hosea 11:9. Where is God in their present reality?

When you feel undone it may be normal to feel alone, but it is still a lie. God is there in the midst of it all. He does not come in wrath, but He brings His holiness and that changes things. Whatever causes you to feel alone, it's time to look toward your future.

Journal Prompt: I can protect myself from following the same pattern of the Israelites by…..

Day 3: Future Realized – Walk On

God has reviewed their past, and reminded them that He is right there with them and that He can never let them go. Now He is going to launch them into the reminder of their inheritance, the future they must raise their eyes and behold so that they can have hope during the difficulties ahead.

Read Hosea 11:10 in various translations. What does God say that His people will do?

You likely found words like follow, walk, go after. It means "to walk, go, come; human locomotion taken without suggestion of a definite destination."

What strikes you most about this definition?

Read Hebrews 11:8. How does this passage support the definition for "walk" above?

Read these verses and record what you learn about how we are to walk.
- Psalm 81:8-16

- Psalm 119:45

How hard it is to follow God when He doesn't make the destination clear! Doesn't this seem like a mistake? This was an exciting and profound lesson for me and I hope it is for you. While I do believe that God calls us to specific and clear action, this is a message for those of His children who are refusing Him because they are undone or unsure. Here it is. Following God, walking with Him, simply means we are together with Him on life's journey. It means we are content to be with Him wherever He leads, regardless of the destination. Remember the toddler God was teaching to walk? It means she grows up and chooses to stay by His side. God is affirming the importance of RELATIONSHIP over RELIGION.

Take a few minutes to look up these verses about walking with God.
- 2 Corinthians 6:16

- Colossians 3:7-8

- 1 John 1:6-7

Write a description of what a woman who walks with God looks like:

We are going to head to our last chapter in Hosea, but first let's review God's reminders for His people from chapter 11.
What did you learn about your past?

What did you learn about your present reality?

What did you learn about your future?

Journal Prompt: As I consider the future, I am most thankful for.....

Day 4: Real Repentance

As we head to our last lessons from this book, there are some looming questions. How do I walk forward with chains falling? How do I get home to Him? I see now that He loves me and that I should be walking with Him, but HOW? The answer in chapter 14 should be one that we practice with ferocity. It might surprise you, just like waiting it is a neglected spiritual discipline. Repentance.

Read Hosea 14. Take time to go to your journal and write a prayerful response to Him.

We touched on a fake apology earlier in our study. Now, how precious is a heartfelt one? When one of my children apologizes on their own and shows true sorrow for the wrong they've done, I want to throw a party! It brings me such delight and I react so strongly that it has, on occasion, caused them confusion. A truly repentant apology doesn't just repair a relationship, it strengthens it.

In Hosea 14 there are six steps in the process of repentance.
1. ***Recognize SIN as your downfall*** (14:1).
Recognition of sin is very unpopular today, but there really is no other place to start. Remember the Godly Yet and extend the same grace to yourself. God loves you too much not to tell you the truth about your sin. Accept no excuses. Don't rationalize. It's abhorrent to Him and to you. But it's not the end of you. Knowing that God's forgiveness is around the corner gives you the courage to face your sin. Do it.

Read Psalm 32:5 and write down what it says to do with sin.

2. *Go to God with WORDS – Say it!* (14:2)

This part of the verse is so precious to me yet I feel the trepidation. Even now, I feel the painful lump in my throat. Sometimes I find myself with God, so burdened about something that I can't speak. When it comes to my sin, that's not enough. Recognizing the burden isn't enough. Hosea says, "take with you words". They don't have to come out with beauty and reason. It's completely ok to ugly cry and just grind out a sincere "I am so sorry." God sees your heart, but still He instructs us to bring words.

Why do you think Hosea tells us to take words with us when we are repenting?

God doesn't need to HEAR the words, He knows that we need to SAY the words. Have you ever tried to describe a confusing problem reluctantly and then found understanding in the words you utter? When it comes to confession this type of Ah-Ha moment is a crucial part of your journey to repentance.

3. *Make your confession SPECIFIC* (14:3)

Read Hosea 14:3 and record the specific things in the apology. Jot down any significance you notice.

By being specific with their apology they address the specific sin of idolatry. They had *specifically* sought alliances with Assyria and strength in implements of warfare when they felt threatened by their enemies. They had *specifically* worshipped false idols when they were afraid God wouldn't provide.

4. *Appeal to His GRACE and understand His forgiveness* (14:2)
What do they ask God in verse 2?

"Take away" literally means "to raise or lift up (the face, the eyes, the voice, or the soul)." Keeping this in mind read Isaiah 53:4,12. These two verses have the same original word for "take away." It may be translated "bore". Rewrite the two verses in Isaiah, using the phrase "Took away."

Who does this describe?

Jesus. There is no salvation, there is no forgiveness, there is no redemption, there is no hope without Him. In a study so deeply connected to the stories and truths of the Old Testament, we mustn't lose sight of Jesus. Even in the Old Testament the people of God who trusted and believed Him were looking toward Jesus (Heb. 11:13). When you go to God with the words of a sincere and specific apology, you appeal to Him through the grace that was shown to you when Jesus took away your sin. He tucks his nail-pierced hand under your chin and lifts your face, waiting for your eyes to meet His, and assures you that you are forgiven. How I love Him.

5. **_Stay ATTACHED to Him for growth_** (14:4-8)
Read Hosea 14:4-8 and describe the miracle.

One of the effects of repentance is that it clears the path for fruitfulness. Read John 15:1-5 and be reminded of the benefit of staying attached to God. How specifically can you do this in your life?

6. **_Keep WALKING in His ways_** (14:9)
The last phrases of this chapter remind me of Dori the fish's song in _Finding Nemo_, "just keep swimming, just keep swimming...." Just keep walking. You've learned how. You know that it's safe to walk with God and that He is trustworthy, so just keep walking.

There is a very unique phrase at the end of Hosea 14:2. In my translation it says, "the vows of our lips." Read this verse in your Bible and look it up in several translations. Write down the different words for "vows" that you find.

Literally this says, "so we will render the calves of our lips."[21] If it weren't such a precious and intimate picture I might be tempted to giggle. I'm all for the sincere apology, but how do we offer calves from our lips?

---

21 (Zodhiates), 2157.

Read Hosea 8:5-6, 10:5, 13:2 and see how God's people have handled sacrifices in their recent history.

They had polluted the original intent of this sacrifice offering with their idolatry. But this image actually refers to the peace offerings that the Israelites would make to God Himself (Exodus 24:5, Numbers 7:88), "in which the grateful worshipper enjoys a meal in God's presence."[22] So miraculous. Please don't miss that this is a peace offering. The people long for peace with God. In the middle of a lesson on how they can return to Him is a reminder of peace. These people have done unspeakable things and have ruined their families and their worship and their relationship with God with destructive sin and still God invites them to dinner. The only note on the invitation says "RSVP with sincere repentance". The cost has already been paid.

Read Hebrews 13:15 and note how we are to offer this peace offering to God.

Journal Prompt: Repentance means…..

---

22   (ESV Study Bible), 1642.

Day 5: Repentance Applied

Take a look back at the list we studied this week. There are 6 steps to repentance taken from Hosea 14. Write them out here:

1.

2.

3.

4.

5.

6.

Read Hosea 6:1-4. This is an account of a shallow confession that isn't acceptable to God. Compare the two confessions using the list from your notes. See if you can determine what's missing from the Hosea 6 confession. Check out Hosea 7:14 for a reminder from God about their fake apologies.

Circle or underline the steps in the Hosea 14 list above that are hardest for you and make them a matter of concentrated prayer. Keep praying about it daily, asking God to help you understand and take action in these areas.

From what I've experienced on my own and observed in ministering to women, there are a couple of places where we get stuck on repentance. We either can't get past a sin from our past and so stay stuck on number four, or we compare our lifestyles to others and feel "good enough" about how we live never even getting started at number one!

If you are refusing to accept God's forgiveness and let go of the past, you're stuck on number four. Look at numbers five and six on the Steps to Repentance list and see what you're missing! Write it out here.

Read the following verses and let go of the past and whatever might be keeping you from accepting God's forgiveness. Remember that Gomer's refusal to accept her true identity as Hosea's wife is what eventually led her to become a slave.

Psalm 103:11-4

2 Corinthians 5:17

1 Corinthians 6:9-11

When I was young, I would've been glad to read these verses but unable to know how much they would apply to me someday. Now that I'm older I better know how complete and transforming God's forgiveness really is. This has become a lifesaving truth that I cling to. His grace is my identity in every way. So even if this lesson doesn't seem to apply to you, take the verses to heart. You never know when you might be able to use these lessons to encourage someone; and you never know what the future holds – there might come a day when you need these reminders of God's grace.

If you are in the second group I mentioned, the "compare your lifestyle to others and feel good enough about how you live so that you never even get started at number one" group, it's your turn. Take this opportunity to examine your life and get serious about living according to God's standard alone. It's always easy for us church girls to find someone else's filthy lifestyle to make ours look clean. You must know, please hear this; I've found myself in both groups and this one is way more dangerous. At least the first group has made it to Step four in our Repentance List! Church Girl might look down on Guilt Girl, but she would be fooling herself. If you are not making genuine repentance a regular part of your life with God because you feel OK about how you're living, you are in danger. I can't overstate it. You are strong in religion and weak in genuine relationship with God.

Ask Him what needs to go from your life, what needs to stay and what needs to be added. Read these passages *slowly and prayerfully,* summarizing what you learn:

Psalm 139:23-24

Job 31:6

Psalm 26:2

1 Thessalonians 2:4

Psalm 143:10

I love that last part of the last verse, "may your Good Spirit lead me on level ground". This is a great good-bye point and my prayer for each of you.

So this is it. We've come to the end of our time together in Hosea. Maybe you remember this from the end of our first day together: "If you leave this study and don't feel that Hosea was written for you, if you don't walk away convinced that God's love is greater than anything else you have loved back, if you don't walk away from this study more confident in God's Word with chains falling as you walk into your future; then this effort is a failure in my eyes." My only goal is that your time in this study has been a success on these terms. Maybe one day we will sit and visit with Gomer during a heavenly tea party and hear the rest of her story. But I suspect we will be completely taken instead with the affections of our Redeemer. He is the beginning and the end, the reason you and I can walk toward the future with smiles gleaming and chains falling.

Journal Prompt: In response to what I've learned I know......

Small Group Guide

If you decide to work through Hosea together in a small group, here are some things I put together for you.

Here's what we would do:

If I were leading a small group through this study I would get everyone together at a set time each week. I would make or ask for help making snacks for our time together. I would consider using music in the weekly sessions too. I've included discussion questions, recipes, and suggested playlists that you can use from week to week if you're into that kind of thing. Even if you just get together and talk through some of your favorite questions in the study and some of the journal entries, you will fill up your time and learn much from one another. If you are the leader; let the women attending talk about what they are learning. Set a great example by being open and transparent in what you share, but don't put anyone on the spot. Let them share as they feel comfortable and compelled on their own. The nature of this study is very personal at some points, so just do what you can to offer support and encouragement to the women who meet with you. You don't have to answer every question that comes up....search together, challenge and comfort one another. More than anything pray for one another every week and throughout the week.

Intro Week Discussion Questions:

- What do you know about the book of Hosea? Find it together using the Table of Contents in your Bibles, consider giving everyone a bookmark to mark the spot.
- What are your first reactions to studying a book on Hosea?

Give everyone a copy of <u>Chains Falling</u> and read the introduction together before you talk about these questions:

- What translation is your Bible? Why do you like it?
- Do you journal? Why or Why not?
- Read the opening passage on Week 1, Day 1 from the Message and share what you think about it.
- Encourage everyone to do the study for Week 1 before you get together next, remind them to keep up in their journals too.

Week 1 Discussion Questions: Prophet Hosea, Husband Hosea

- Retell Hosea and Gomer's story together. Was this new to you?
- What are the similarities between our culture and Hosea's?
- What are your reactions to Gomer?
- Brainstorm together some lies that we tend to accept as truth. How do these beliefs become our idols?
- Review Isaiah 44:9-10 from Day 4 and share your favorite cross-references.
- After studying idolatry, are there any things that need to go from your life?
- How did you react to the names of Gomer's children?
- Ask for volunteers to share their journal entry on Day 5.

Week 1 Suggested Playlist:

Orphans of God – Avalon
Who Am I? – Casting Crowns
Embracing Accusations – Shane and Shane

Week 2 Discussion Questions: God's People Passion

- The Godly Yet is one of the key teachings from the book of Hosea. What is it?
- Ask for volunteers to share journal entries for Day 1.
- When has God changed your Trouble into Hope?
- Review the verses that talk about God's grief on Day 3. What do you think about this concept?
- Read the statement *"BLESSED! are ALL of you when you wait!"* out loud with the "particle of exclamation" emphasis you learned in Day 4.
- Try to empathize with those who fell into Baal worship. What might've led them there?
- What are the ways that you move ahead of God, calling for Him to follow you? Do you think this is idolatry?

Week 2 Suggested Playlist:

You Never Let Go – Matt Redman
Never Let Go – David Crowder
Moving All the While – Sidewalk Prophets

Week 3 Discussion Questions: Redemption

- Review what you learned about God's disciplining love from Hebrews 12:7-12.
- What is the difference in a hedge of protection and a hedge of boundary?
- Talk about what it must've been like for Gomer to be bought by Hosea. Put yourself in her shoes and really paint the scene together.

- Review the instructions Hosea gives Gomer after he buys her *(Hosea 3:3)* and discuss together why he says the specific things we read there.
- Ask for volunteers to read their journal entries for Day 3.
- Read the *"Jamy Paraphrase"* of Isaiah 50:1-2 from Day 4 and discuss your reactions to it.
- What does it mean to be redeemed?
- Ask for volunteers to share their journal entries for Day 5.

Week 3 Suggested Playlist:

Unredeemed – Selah
There is a Fountain – Selah
Mercy – Casting Crowns
Beautiful for Me – Nichole Nordeman

Week 4 Discussion Questions: The Case Against God's People

- Discuss the concept of spiritual amnesia. Can you see this in our culture?
- Which of the three parts of spiritual amnesia give you the most trouble?
- Read Judges 2:10 and Psalm 78:5-8 and discuss our responsibility to the next generation.
- What did you learn from your research working for the prosecution on Day 2?
- Discuss the 5 areas of influence listed in 1Timothy 4:12.
- What did you think about the teaching on desire from Day 4? How does this impact your thinking about repentance?
- What is your plan to remember God from Day 5? *Summary of the Deuteronomy verses.*

Week 4 Suggested Playlist:

Healing is in Your Hands – Christy Nockels

How Deep the Father's Love for Us – Stuart Townsend, arr. Travis Cottrell
Somewhere in the Middle – Casting Crowns

Week 5 Discussion Questions: Coming Home

- Ask for volunteers to share their journal entries from Day 1.
- What are some ways that you are sowing the wind?
- Review the losses from Day 2. Which ones bothered you the most?
- What are we to do in the process of coming home?
- Did you learn anything new about waiting? Where are you struggling to wait on God right now?
- Which is your favorite aspect of God's responsibility in our homecoming?
- Review Isaiah 26:8 and take a few minutes just to marvel, add in some happy sighs before you all go home.

Week 5 Suggested Playlist:

Not Guilty – Mandisa
While I'm Waiting – John Waller
Beautiful Exchange - Transparency

Week 6 Discussion Questions: Walk On with Repentance on Your Mind

- Have someone in your group model the Father/Toddler walk illustrated in Hosea 11:3-4. How precious is this to you?
- What patterns did you see in Psalm 106?
- Share what makes you feel undone. How do you cope with this feeling?

- Ask for volunteers to share their journal entries for Day 3.
- What did you learn about sincere repentance that you didn't know before?
- Look at Day 5 together. Make a visible list of the 6 steps to repentance. Discuss the two types of getting stuck mentioned in Day 5. Offer support and accountability to one another as you commit to walking on with God.
- Review the goals for the study written in italics at the end of Day 5. Share how this study was a success for you personally. What did you learn?

Week 6 Suggested Playlist:

Change This Heart – Sidewalk Prophets
I'm Moving On – Jeff Johnson
Restless – Audrey Assad

Favorite Recipes

I'm not sure when your small group will be getting together; mine is a morning group so we eat breakfast together every Wednesday morning. Here are some of my favorite breakfast and snack recipes. Enjoy!

Favorite Salsa

Adapted from an Austin Jr. League Cookbook my brother-in-law gave me.
1 large can whole tomatoes
1 fresh jalapeno pepper, *remove seeds from half to control heat*
½ small or medium onion
2 teaspoons salt
1 teaspoon ground cumin
2 Tablespoons lime juice
½ teaspoon sugar
1 Tablespoon fresh cilantro
1 ½ teaspoons minced garlic (or about 2 cloves fresh)
Put everything in blender after coarse chopping onions and pepper. Blend well. Allow to sit in fridge for several hours or overnight. Can substitute stewed tomatoes, omitting sugar from recipe.

Amanda's Guacamole

4 avocados
4 grape tomatoes
¼ red onion
Garlic salt
Lime juice
Peel and smash the avocados. Dice up tomatoes and onion. Stir into the avocado. Add garlic salt and lime juice to taste. Stir and serve.

Apple Brickle Dip

1 package cream cheese (8 oz.), softened
½ cup brown sugar
¼ cup white sugar
1 teaspoon vanilla
1 package almond brickle chips (toffee)
Blend cream cheese, sugars and vanilla well. Add entire bag of brickle chips, stir well. Refrigerate. Set out about 30 minutes before serving time to soften. Serve with granny smith apple chunks or slices.

Ashley's Peanut Butter Popcorn

½ cup sugar
¼ cup honey
¼ cup light corn syrup
½ cup peanut butter
½ teaspoon vanilla
½ cup popcorn (or 2 bags microwave)
Pop popcorn and put in a large bowl, picking out any unpopped kernels. In a medium saucepan bring sugar, honey, and corn syrup to a boil. Remove from heat and add peanut butter and vanilla. Stir well and pour entire mixture over popcorn. Stir to coat, pour out on waxed paper to cool.

Dianna's Sweet and Salty

Mix together in a very large bowl:
- 10 ounce package mini pretzels
- 5 cups cheerios
- 5 cups corn chex
- 2 cups salted peanuts
- 1 pound M&M candy

Melt together in microwave:
- 2 packages white chocolate chips (12 oz each)
- 3 tablespoons canola or vegetable oil

Pour over dry ingredients, stir to cover and pour out onto waxed paper to cool and set.

Pistachio Almond Sugar Cookies

2/3 cup shortening
2/3 cup sugar
2 eggs
½ teaspoon vanilla
½ teaspoon almond extract
½ teaspoon salt
1 pistachio almond pudding mix
2 cups flour

Mix shortening and sugar together well, add eggs, and extracts. Add salt, pudding mix and flour. Mix well. Scoop into small balls and bake for 8 minutes at 375 degrees. Frost with store bought butter cream icing and sprinkles. Makes 3 dozen.

Blueberry Muffins

From Pam Anderson's book, <u>The Perfect Recipe</u>
3 cups flour
1 Tablespoon baking powder
½ teaspoon baking soda
½ teaspoon salt
10 Tablespoons butter–at room temperature
1 cup sugar
2 large eggs
1 ½ cups plain or vanilla yogurt
1 ½ cup blueberries tossed with 1 T. Flour OR mini chocolate chips
Preheat oven to 350 degrees. Coat 18 muffin cups with cooking spray or line with paper liners. Mix flour, baking powder, baking soda, and salt in a medium bowl and set aside. Beat butter and sugar with an electric mixer until light and fluffy. Add eggs and beat well. Beat in half of the dry ingredients followed by ½ of the yogurt just until barely incorporated. Beat in remaining dry ingredients followed by remaining yogurt just until incorporated. Stir in blueberries or mini chocolate chips. Divide evenly between muffin cups and bake for 20 - 25 minutes.

Chocolate–Chocolate Chip Muffins

1 package chocolate fudge cake mix
1 small box instant chocolate pudding mix
¾ cup water
4 eggs, beaten
½ cup oil
1 cup mini chocolate chips, frozen
½ tsp. Almond extract
Mix cake mix, pudding, water, eggs, oil and almond extract until smooth. Stir in chocolate chips. Fill 18 greased and paper lined muffin cups, bake for 25 minutes at 350 degrees.

Sausage Strata

This recipe came from the family I mentioned in Week 2 Day 3. It was oft-requested where I grew up.

6-8 slices bread, cubed
1 pound sausage, cooked and drained
2 cups milk (originally 1 ¼ cup milk and ¾ cup half and half)
1 teaspoon dry mustard
1 teaspoon Worcestershire Sauce
½ cup grated Cheddar Cheese – I use more, the original called for Velveeta
5 eggs, lightly beaten
Mix well, bake in a greased 9x13 at 350 degrees for 35-45 minutes. This is GREAT to make the night before, let sit in the fridge overnight and then bake in the morning, bake for 45 minutes.

Christmas Cappuccino

5-6 cinnamon sticks
½ cup Folger's instant coffee
¾ cup sugar
6 cups boiling water
3 cups half and half
1 teaspoon vanilla extract
½ teaspoon almond extract
Put cinnamon sticks, coffee and sugar in a large saucepan. Pour boiling water (10 minutes in microwave) over mixture and stir. Cover and allow to sit for about 5 minutes. Meanwhile heat half and half (3 minutes in microwave). Add to coffee mixture and heat to a low simmer. Add extracts and serve. This works great in a pump pot because the pot gives it a foamy top. Top with whipping cream, chocolate shavings or crushed candy canes or cinnamon.
Makes 1 pump pot (about 15 servings).

Works Cited

Boice, James Montgomery. The Minor Prophets, Volume 1. Grand Rapids, Michigan: Baker Books, 1983.

Butler, Trent C. Holman Bible Dictionary. Holman Bible Publishers, 1991.

ESV Study Bible. Good News Publishers, 2008.

Zodhiates, Spiros. The Complete Word Study Old Testament. AMG Publishers, 1994.

CPSIA information can be obtained at www.ICGtesting.com
Printed in the USA
LVOW121409261211

260937LV00001B/21/P